BUILDING A NEW JAPAN

A Plan for
Remodeling the Japanese Archipelago

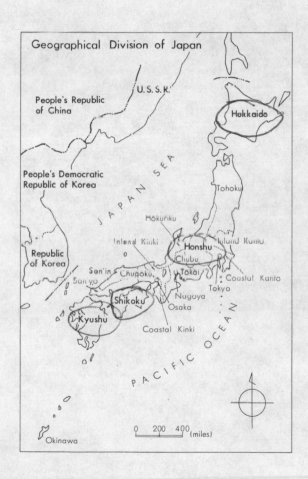

Geographical Division of Japan

BUILDING
A NEW JAPAN

A Plan for
Remodeling the Japanese Archipelago

Prime Minister of Japan
KAKUEI TANAKA

translated by Simul International

THE SIMUL PRESS, INC.
Tokyo, Japan

Copyright © 1972 by Kakuei Tanaka
First English edition May, 1973
2nd printing July, 1973

THE SIMUL PRESS, INC.
Kowa Daisan Bldg., 1-11-45, Akasaka, Minato-ku, Tokyo 107,
Japan

Printed in Japan by Toppan Printing Co., Ltd.
Calligraphy by Kakuei Tanaka
Jacket design by Susumu Tada
JBC 0031-130013-2703

2/22/74 - $12.95

For the English Edition

Kakuei Tanaka

The Japanese edition of this book was published in June, 1972, shortly before I assumed the post of the Prime Minister of Japan. In it I set forth my own concrete ideas for the remodeling of the Japanese archipelago, ideas born of my twenty-five years of service to developing our land. This vision, as well as the policy package for realizing it, has today produced a nationwide debate beyond all expectations. Over the long run, I believe such debate constitutes the primary motive force for improving the political and economic structure of our nation.

The rapid economic growth of postwar Japan, particularly since the mid-1950's, has spurred industrialization and urbanization throughout the nation. The result has been the excessive concentration of both population and industry in the Tokyo-Nagoya-Osaka belt along the Pacific coast, forming a hyper-dense community the likes of which is not to be found elsewhere in the world.

All of the major industrial nations of the world are today faced with the common agonies of inflation, urban deterioration, environmental pollution, stagnant agriculture, and spiritual frustration amidst material affluence. This is especially so in Japan. Smaller than the single state of California, Japan has nearly one-third of the people concentrated on a mere one percent of the land, making the tempo of social and economic change so much the greater.

What I have done here is to launch a realistic action program aimed at a sweeping revision of land uses embodying as its main tools nationwide industrial relocation and the formation of national information and communications networks, so that we Japanese may solve the immediate difficulties facing us and may be able to create a spiritually affluent life in pleasant surroundings. My book is a blueprint for this grand design.

The world has begun its turn away from the long years of division and confrontation and toward a new era of coexistence and international cooperation. In such a changing world, Japan must contribute positively to realization of a better and more prosperous life for all of mankind in a spirit of fairness and social justice. As the Japanese people press forward with this national remodeling, I have no doubt that our goals of global peace and national welfare will be better understood by other peoples, and that we will become better neighbors and lasting friends. I will be doubly delighted if the prescriptions I have proposed for Japan prove to be of interest to other nations.

Finally I would like to pay my respects and express my heartfelt appreciation to Mr. Katsuo Tamura and his staff at The Simul Press, Inc., and to Mr. Masumi Muramatsu and his staff at Simul International, Inc., for having proposed and planned the publication of this English-language edition of my book and for having carried the project to completion so superbly. (Tokyo, April 1973)

PREFACE

As certain as water flowing downward, man ever seeks newer heights. Modern economic history of many countries shows a flow of population from primary to secondary to tertiary industries, from rural areas to urban centers, a flow which has increased GNP and national income. The flow of people in search of higher incomes and a better life has served as the driving force in the creation of modern civilization. Japan is no exception. Its rapid growth in the century following the Meiji Restoration has been in direct proportion to its industrialization and urbanization.

But the rapid economic growth that began in the last half of the 1950's brought about an excessive concentration of population and industry along the Pacific coast, transforming Japan into a unique society of high population density. While the big cities suffer from the pains and irritations of overcrowding, rural areas suffer from the exodus of youth and the resultant loss of vital energy for growth. Rapid urbanization has bred increasing numbers of people who have never known the joys of rural life, chasing rabbits in mountains, fishing for crucians in streams, whose only home is a tiny apartment in some huge city. With such a situation, how can we pass on to future generations the qualities and traditions of the Japanese people?

At this centennial point of the Meiji Restoration, the advantages of urban concentration are clearly being overwhelmed by the disadvantages. Public opinion calls for the simultaneous solution of overcrowding and underpopulation to live in comfort in a beautiful land of affluence and security. To achieve these ends, we must boldly reverse this torrential urban concentration and direct our national energy and surplus economic strength to remodeling the entire archipelago. Disparity between urban and rural areas, between the prosperous Pacific coast and the stagnating Japan Sea coast, can surely be eliminated by using levers such as relocating industries, making them more knowledge-intensive, constructing super-express railways and trunk expressways throughout the nation, and creating nationwide information and communication networks.

Whether or not Japan can follow a path of peace and international cooperation in an open world economy depends upon its successful and positive reform of domestic industrial and regional economic structure. In this sense, the remodeling of the Japanese archipelago is the most important domestic task for Japan. I am determined to devote myself to this task, to spreading communities throughout the nation where industry, culture, and nature are in harmony, and thereby achieving for Japan a society in which all of us may be proud.

In March of 1972, I had the honor of being given an award by the House of Representatives for my long service in that body. It was this occasion which prompted me to review the path I have followed in the last quarter century in the interest of national development and solving urban problems, and to attempt to present before the public my own prescriptions from an entirely new perspective for remodeling the Japanese archipelago. I shall be most pleased if this proves useful and interesting to my fellow countrymen as well as to those concerned.

Finally, I would like to express my deep appreciation to the staff of the Nikkan Kogyo Shimbun, Ltd. (Industrial Daily News, Ltd.) and the experts of various Ministries and Agencies concerned for their devoted efforts and cooperation which have made this book possible.

Kakuei Tanaka

Mejiro-dai, Tokyo
June, 1972

CONTENTS

PART II
Rechanneling the Flow of People and Economy

PART III
Urban Remodeling and Regional Development

Commentary:
Kakuei Tanaka and His *Building a New Japan*

Prefectures of Japan

Prefectural capitals

① Sapporo
② Aomori
③ Morioka
④ Akita
⑤ Sendai
⑥ Yamagata
⑦ Fukushima
⑧ Niigata
⑨ Mito
⑩ Utsunomiya
⑪ Chiba
⑫ Urawa
⑬ Tokyo
⑭ Yokohama
⑮ Maebashi
⑯ Nagano
⑰ Kofu
⑱ Shizuoka
⑲ Toyama
⑳ Kanazawa
㉑ Fukui
㉒ Gifu
㉓ Nagoya
㉔ Otsu

㉕ Tsu
㉖ Kyoto
㉗ Nara
㉘ Osaka
㉙ Wakayama
㉚ Kobe
㉛ Tottori
㉜ Okayama
㉝ Matsue
㉞ Hiroshima
㉟ Yamaguchi
㊱ Takamatsu
㊲ Tokushima
㊳ Matsuyama
㊴ Kochi
㊵ Fukuoka
㊶ Saga
㊷ Nagasaki
㊸ Oita
㊹ Kumamoto
㊺ Miyazaki
㊻ Kagoshima
㊼ Naha

For Japan's Tomorrow

The Meiji Centennial as a Turning Point

On March 7, 1972, twelve colleagues of mine and I were awarded an honor by the House of Representatives for our long years of service in the Diet. By then, I had served in the Diet for twenty-five years since being elected to the House of Representatives in the first national election under the new Constitution. In retrospect, this quarter century of my life has been at one with the history of postwar national development. But my work is not over by any means. The remodeling of the Japanese archipelago is only now to start.

The centennial of the 1868 Meiji Restoration fell precisely at the point where the advantages of urban concentration began to be outweighed by the disadvantages. While the big cities are suffering from overcrowding, pollution, and rising prices, the outlying areas are growing desolate through the exodus of population. The disparity between urban and rural areas, between the Pacific coast and the Japan Sea coast, is now at an all-time high. This state of affairs requires drastic improvement. During my quarter century in politics, I have consistently sought to construct a society where both the people in the cities and the people on the farms can live comfortable lives which are spiritually worth living.

It seems to me that my first major policy-making contribution to national development was the drafting of the Comprehensive National Land Development Act in 1950, only five years after the end of the War.

Following the establishment of this basic law for future land development policies, I took the initiative in revising the Road Law, introducing the toll road system, establishing the gasoline tax, amending the River Law, and enacting the Water Resources Development Promotion Law. This brought me up to 1968 when I took the lead in drafting "The General Principles of Urban Policy," so named because urban problems had finally been taken up by the mass media and academia and had begun to attract a strong popular interest.

This document did not set forth an urban policy in the narrow sense of the term but stated general principles for comprehensive national remodeling which were based upon a conception of the entire country as an integral and urban whole. As such, it covers a wide range of subjects. Here I would like to explain the five principal points emphasized in its Preamble, because they represent a concise statement of my thinking on the remodeling of the nation.

Five Focal Points

The first is to establish a new national land program, and to improve legal and administrative mechanisms for the execution of the program.

The new national land program set basic objectives of policy for each specific area, such as industrial development, natural and living environments, and trunk transportation networks. It also established for each region comprehensive development goals, combining land uses, population, water supply, and other essentials. The legal system suggested would be based upon an overall revision of the Comprehensive National Land Development Act, modifying or abolishing today's overcomplicated legal system. It also envisioned a central administrative body to be established for the vigorous execution of development policies. At the same time there would be an effort to strengthen broad regional administrative systems, including a thorough review in the future of the present prefectural system. New super-express railway lines tying the nation together would be constructed throughout the nation. A national development research center would be established.

The second point is to free urban residents, especially those in the metropolitan areas, from housing problems, traffic hazards, and pollution. For this purpose, under the Japanese adage of "living near work or working near home," urban redevelopment would be selectively carried out by "three-dimensionalizing" our flat cities, at the same time systematically developing suburbia and constructing new cities. This would be accomplished partly by supplying large quantities of high quality, high-rise apartments. The participation of private developers would be sought as the primary force for this construction. Railways, especially subways, would be extended to ease commuter traffic. The principle of "the beneficiary bears the burden" and the system of "the polluter pays" would be firmly established.

The third point of emphasis is to base local development on a new formula of focal-point development, by strengthening strategically located focal cities in different regions and by constructing large industrial bases.

To effectively connect the focal points with the cities and villages of their hinterlands, large concentrations of fiscal funds would be required to build industrial and social infrastructures such as roads, as pump-priming investments. In order to raise the income of the local areas to a level equal to urban Japan, secondary and tertiary industries should be located there as well. The agricultural land system should be reexamined thoroughly to help develop an attractive, modern rural life by encouraging highly productive and profitable kinds of agriculture and self-sufficiency of food supply. Special attention should also be paid to increasing production of livestock and fruit in response to shifts in agricultural supply and demand.

The fourth point is to establish plans and methods of land utilization under the basic philosophy of giving priority to the public interest. The plans would provide for the appropriate location of cities, for securing good industrial and agricultural sites, and for the protection of nature. Especially in big cities, disorderly development would be prevented by making zoning regulations designating areas for urbanization and other specific purposes. This zoning system would be applied fully to secure the land necessary for roads and other public uses. Efficient land

4

utilization from the regional and national standpoint would be promoted by the establishment of a land committee. This committee would have the power to make emergency decisions on land expropriation and to ensure uniformity in assessing and pricing land.

The fifth point of emphasis deals with securing the necessary capital resources for this national remodeling by utilizing the funds and savings of the entire population. Concentrated investment for development should be possible without causing inflation if private investment capital is brought in by making full use of the Government's fiscal and monetary tools and strengthening the interest supplement system. Urban redevelopment banks would be established as focal financial institutions, providing large sums of low-interest, long-term capital for various aspects of the remodeling.

While this summarizes the five main points of emphasis, let us examine "The General Principles of Urban Policy" a little further to review such basic issues as how this national rebuilding relates to the functioning of the fiscal system, the basic source of capital; what problems, if any, arise in relation to local governments; and its implications in regard to the present agricultural land system.

Fiscal Policy for Remodeling the Nation

Let us take up the fiscal problems first. During the past one hundred years, Japan has placed primary emphasis on fiscal policy under which resource allocation through fiscal means has played a central role in guiding the economy, with the taxation system playing only a complementary role. Clearly, the time has arrived to correct this pattern. While the emphasis on fiscal measures was appropriate for a developing nation, we are now on the verge of beginning a new century as a major industrial nation and should make more effective use of the taxation system. More effective taxation and more efficient and farsighted use of fiscal funds would constitute two of the main pillars of the remodeling effort.

So far, the criterion for fiscal investment has been past performance. For example, "Specific Important Ports" are designated for funding on the basis of how much cargo they have handled in the past. This method of operation has not only prevented policy from playing its intended role but has consequently contributed to inflated budgets. This passive fiscal approach cannot be permitted if our remodeling is to be successful. Remodeling is to serve as the forerunner of the future, and naturally requires colossal capital outlays for such projects as improving the entire transportation network. This is what I mean by the pump-priming uses of fiscal policy.

Along with this, the taxation system, which has so far played only a supplemental role, should now come into positive play. In order to curtail urban functions of the big cities and to accelerate local development, the political adjustment functions of the taxation system should be used effectively to discourage some activities and promote others. The wealth accumulated and profits realized over the years in developing the big cities should be thought of as a source of capital for financing the new nation-building under the "beneficiary bears the burden" and the "polluter pays" principles. In conjunction with this, we should also be flexible in providing tax benefits or exemptions for such projects as the construction of high-rise apartment buildings.

At the same time, in outlying areas where no such benefits of accumulation exist, drastic preferential measures must be adopted to facilitate improvement in the residential and industrial infrastructures as well as to bring in new industries. Specifically, electricity rates should be different for overcrowded and underpopulated areas; similar policy consideration should be given for the industrial water supply; resident taxes should be lowered in areas of sparse population; and businesses building new factories in underdeveloped areas should be exempted, in whole or in part, from municipal property taxes for twenty-five years, with the local governments subsidized by the national government to cover the costs of such preferential treatment. Such multifaceted policy measures should be studied and eventually realized.

In any case, an enormous amount of money will be required for remodeling. The fiscal resources of the national government alone could not possibly be sufficient. These must be supplemented by private resources which can be mobilized by creating a setup in accord with monetary mechanisms. The interest supplement system is one powerful means to bring in private capital. The funds of insurance companies, life and casualty, of trust and savings banks, and of agricultural cooperatives should be mobilized for the building of a new Japan.

Public bonds should be issued as an integral part of such financing. Instead of trying to balance the budget each fiscal year, there should be planned, positive bond flotations in accordance with long-term fiscal plans to facilitate the accumulation of social overhead capital for the prosperity of future generations.

Coordination with Local Governments

Will this create any complications with local governments? The answer is that, if the new remodeling program is executed in complete coordination with local government planning at all levels, there will be no conflict with national policy. Given the continuing expansion of socio-economic spheres, local development not in keeping with national plans cannot survive for long. Conversely, no national plans can be realized without the support of local development. In this sense, the role of local government in Japan's rebuilding is highly significant. If the entire archipelago is to be remodeled so that all areas can be brought within a one-day sphere in terms of traveling and economic distance, local administrative units must be enlarged. As a first step, cities, towns, and villages should be combined, strengthening them as basic local units. This could be accomplished by proceeding with the second round of consolidation to make them the proper size and to give them sufficient administrative and fiscal authority. Adjacent cities should be reorganized to permit larger metropolitan units for inter-city administrative coordination and the sharing of services on a wider scale.

Such measures are necessary because developments in the means of transportation and communication, and the resultant flow of people and goods, have rapidly expanded living and economic spheres across prefectural boundaries. Additionally, broader regional administration must be furthered in order to solve such problems as land utilization, water resource development, housing, traffic, pollution, and education.

The problem here is with the present prefectural system, which goes back one century to the beginning of the Meiji Era when the provinces of old feudal clans were replaced by prefectures. My conclusion is that prefectures under the present system are administrative units of a rather ambiguous nature, floating somewhere between the national and the city-town-village level. This system is not conducive to future economic development or broader regional administration. It is time to reconsider the present prefectural system in view of future needs, even including basic reform or abolition.

One idea would be to establish new broad regional bodies to provide an intermediate level of administration between the national and local levels. Such regional governments could absorb many administrative tasks entrusted to prefectural governments by the national government and could take over the operation of national government branch offices, thus relieving the prefectural governments of about two-thirds of their current workload. The result would be a more unified administration on the regional level, one somewhat better able to cope with rapidly changing economic and social institutions.

Effects on Farmland Policy

Another big problem is the implications of the remodeling plan for present agricultural land policy.

In 1960, Japan's agricultural population was 13,560,000, or 31 percent of the total work force. By 1971, this declined to 7,680,000 or 15.9 percent, and two-thirds of them were elderly people, women, or people incapable of strenuous physical labor. From the first year of the Meiji Era (1868) until 1952, about 400,000 people joined the agricultural labor force each year. This fell to only 42,000 in 1969, 37,000 in 1970, and a mere 32,000 in 1971, dwindling to less than 10 percent of the figure of only two decades ago.

As our economy becomes more open and our industrial structure more advanced, it is absolutely necessary to make our agriculture more efficient and profitable if we are to compete with overseas agricultural products and to secure a stable self-sufficiency in foodstuffs, one in accord with changing Japanese dietary habits. For this purpose, it is necessary to mechanize our agriculture and organize it more efficiently.

Looking forward to the year 1985, when the per-capita GNP is expected to reach $8,000, the percentage of the total population engaged in agriculture will inevitably decline to about 4 to 6 percent, the average for the world's ten most advanced industrial countries. In such a situation, the ideal arrangement for agriculture would be for each farming unit to cultivate 2.5 acres of owned land and 25 to 50 acres of leased land. But in view of the present pattern of scattered and minuscule land ownership and high land prices, it is extremely difficult to enlarge the scale of individual farm management. Because of this, the driving force behind agriculture of the future will be cooperatives, subcontractors, and salaried cultivators.

Only when the economic structure becomes more sophisticated, permitting farm families to join secondary or tertiary industries and become mere land owners, allowing their small plots of land to be combined, will it be possible to reform Japanese agriculture. Thus it is necessary to establish a nation-wide comprehensive land utilization plan, to set up "permanent farmlands" through coordination between national and local governments, and to abolish the present Agricultural Land Law so as to revive the free flow of farmland, retaining, however, private ownership of agricultural land by farmers. In other words, it is essential to revise the present agricultural land policy in keeping with the national remodeling plan. It goes without saying that legislation should be passed to insure that no land improved with government financial assistance is used for non-agricultural purposes. So this summarizes my proposals.

While rural areas are places of productive work as well as life for agricultural workers, they are at the same time the spiritual home and the recreational ground of the Japanese people. Man cannot survive if completely separated from nature. In order to recharge the energy of our hard-working people in this unique country, this super-densely populated and huge administered society, it is of critical importance to protect our air, water, and vegetation from pollution's poisons and development's devastation so that the people may enjoy nature's beauty at all times. Let me emphasize, therefore, that mountains, forests, grasslands, lakes, and seacoasts all should be carefully preserved, and that lodging and recreational facilities for people should be provided according to an integrated plan.

In my "General Principles of Urban Policy," I discussed key issues such as fiscal institution, local autonomy, and the agricultural land system. What I would like to see is a 180-degree reorientation of our conventional philosophy in order to seek solutions to problems from fresh perspectives.

Legislative Efforts to Date

It may be said that the fundamental idea contained in "The General Principles of Urban Policy" embodies the results of my numerous legislative efforts from the earliest seeds of ideas, nourished over the years, and brought at last to fruition. Therefore, I would like to retrace my footsteps, explaining my thinking as it evolved to become the General Principles.

The first stage was a series of legislation for land development. In 1949, I established the Local Development Subcommittee within the National Planning Committee (presently the Construction Committee) of the House of Representatives and sponsored basic discussions concerning development of power resources which led to the enactment of the Comprehensive National Land Development Law in 1950. While this Law was formally proposed by the Cabinet, it actually originated with my committee. Soon after this start, I worked toward the passage of the Power Resources Development Law, which was also Diet-sponsored. It was just at this time that the Occupation authorities, pursuant to the demilitarization policy, were about to remove as reparations in kind industrial facilities which would enable Japan to rearm, such as precision machinery and heavy and chemical industries. Power development was no exception. Our views were diametrically opposed to those of the Occupation authorities, and ultimately we succeeded in bringing them around to our point of view. Of course, it required considerable courage on our part to resist the almighty authority of SCAP at that time. Perhaps it was my youthful energy that gave me the necessary extra courage.

After we won the argument to develop our own electric power, the next step taken to revive our war-devastated economy and to spur it towards independence and growth was to improve the transportation network. Although Japan's GNP had always grown in proportion with the pace of railroad construction, I felt that roads would become increasingly important as the next transport network. The National Planning Committee in the House of Representatives accordingly took up a basic revision of the 1919 Road Law. The current Road Law, providing the basic underpinnings for all other legislation, was thus sponsored by members of the Diet, including myself, and was enacted in 1952. This revision pivoted on the introduction of the toll road system which marked a radical departure from the prewar principle stipulating that roads should be open to the public free of charge. This toll road system was also clearly originated in the Diet, although it too was first formally proposed by the Cabinet.

The second step was the adoption of the controversial gasoline tax as a special-purpose tax. This tax was proposed as part of the Temporary Measures Law Concerning Funds, etc. of Expenses for Road Improvement (since superseded by the Law Concerning Emergency Measures for Improvement of Roads under the Five-Year Road Improvement Plan), promulgated together with the new Road Law. This was a landmark in the history of Japanese taxation. Academic circles, however, objected to this law, claiming that it was unconstitutional because it interfered with the exclusive right of the Cabinet to formulate budget proposals. My position was that there was no constitutional issue involved, and I stood firmly behind the bill. There was a prolonged debate in both the House of Representatives and the House of Councilors of the Diet of 1952, especially in the upper house where the debate went on for one hundred days. During this time I assumed the entire burden of answering all questions until the bill was finally passed by the Diet. This law states clearly that "the Government shall appropriate for road improvement a sum equal to or greater than the amount of gasoline tax revenue in the fiscal year concerned." Twenty years have passed since then, and this incident has become history, but it remains one of my unforgettable memories today.

Since the gasoline tax was earmarked for road construction and improvement, the financial resources for roads have increased more than one hundred fold from the vicinity of $65 million allocated annually only fifteen years ago. The annual rate of growth of road expenditures was 10.4 percent between 1954 and 1964, precisely in parallel with the rate of Japan's economic growth. In this sense, we may say that Japan's post-war economic recovery began with the three laws concerning roads.

The third step was to legislate for urban development, as for example in the Public-Operated Housing Law. The National Capital Region Development Law served as the driving force for Tokyo's recovery and development. This Law originated in the National Capital Construction Law drafted by the National Planning Committee of the House of Representatives. In those days, there were other similar laws such as the Law for Construction of the International Sight-Seeing, Hot Spring, and Cultural City of Atami, the Law for Transformation of Old Military Port Cities, and the Law for the Construction of the International Sight-Seeing and Cultural City of Kyoto. This National Capital Region Development Law was the forerunner of such other laws that followed as the Act for the Promotion of the Industrial Development of Underdeveloped Regions, the Act for the Promotion of the New Industrial Cities, and the Act for the Development of Special Areas for Industrial Consolidation, and proved indispensable in promoting Japan's economic recovery. Various other laws, each in its own way designed to encourage regional development in Hokkaido, Tohoku, Hokuriku, Shikoku, Chugoku, and Kyushu, were also enacted, and their interaction served as the impetus for the postwar economic recovery.

The revision of the River Law and the enactment of the Water Resources Development Promotion Law were particularly important within this framework.

The River Law, enacted in 1896, provides the basic legal framework for all legislation relating to our waters. It was partially revised in 1951, and wholly revised again in 1964. The partial revision of 1951 was primarily intended for national development and economic growth, but is of special significance in having set forth the general principle that the party responsible for necessitating any construction must bear its costs.

Prior to the revision, all river-related constructions were legally permitted only as temporary structures. If, for example, river banks were to be raised, the costs of dismantling and reconstructing bridges on that river had to be borne, in principle, by the owners of those structures, in this case private railway companies, for example. Since the revision, however, such costs are borne by the state as owner of the river, thus relieving private interests of this burden. This is one of the major reasons that private railway fares are only about four hundred times 1934 or 1936 figures while the general price index shows a 1,000-fold increase. The revision of the River Law thus served to hold down such utility charges. While nobody would question this philosophy today, it would have been absolutely inconceivable in the days of the old Meiji Constitution. Even in 1951, it signaled a unique change in the thinking of the Government. The Water Resources Development Promotion Law was next, enacted in November, 1961. As Chairman of the Special Committee on Water Resources Development, I initiated consideration of this bill, and it was, in fact, our bill, even though it took the form of a Cabinet bill. Although the sharp differences of opinion among the Ministries of Construction, International Trade and Industry, Agriculture and Forestry, and Transport presented serious challenges to me as mediator, the basic importance of water resources for Japan's economic growth served as a unifying factor for all Ministries, and we finally managed to get it through the Committee. It later gave rise to the Water Resources Development Public Corporation Law, the Special Account Law for Flood Control, and even the Special Account for Ports Law and the Foreign Trade Port Development Authority Law. When the Ministry of Finance opposed the Special Account for Flood Control, saying that "no special account lacking specific revenue sources can be allowed under the provisions of the Fiscal Law," my rebuttal was that "water is the biggest revenue resource, and the users of water should pay for it, except for farmers who enjoy vested rights." At long last, this won over the Finance Ministry to pave the way for the special water accounts.

Under the Meiji Constitution, it had been thought that all costs of supplying water and developing port facilities should come from taxes, but this attitude did not result in either adequate development of water resources or improvement of port facilities. Thus I introduced a complete about-face in policy and supported the principle of "beneficiary bears the burden." While it is obviously logical for merchants using port facilities, for example, importing ore and exporting products abroad, to bear some of the costs of providing for these facilities rather than to have the general population bear their entire costs, there was strong opposition at that time, and some people even went so far as to castigate me for my departure from tradition. One hears no such talk these days, as the time for these new ideas has finally come.

The Paradox of Affluence

As the necessary legislative basis for Japan's economic recovery was laid, we entered the period of rapid expansion with the annual growth rate surpassing 10 percent. The average real growth rate between 1954 and 1964 was 10.4 percent, and the corresponding figure during the 1960's was 11.1 percent. This means an overall average growth rate of 10.4 percent during the seventeen years from 1954 through 1970. This was made possible by the industry of the Japanese people and the skilled guidance of the Government. As the entire world looked on in wonder, this high growth rate gave Japan the second largest GNP in the free world, exceeded only by the U.S. Actually, the U.S. is so far out in front that it is more accurate to say that the U.S. is number one and that Japan is sixth with all the positions in between vacant, but at least we have passed West Germany for "sixth" place. If one takes the exchange rate of ¥360 to the dollar, Japan's GNP is more than $200 billion, and with the new rate of ¥308 to the dollar it comes to $230 billion. Either way, it compares favorably with West Germany's $180 billion GNP.

Postwar Japan has experienced three stages of economic development, from the hand-to-mouth existence immediately after our defeat in the War, then rapid growth, and then the internationalization of the economy. Today's prosperity is the result of economic management for growth spurred on by private investment in plants and equipment and the nation-wide urbanization in terms of both population and industry. But it is also true that, at this centennial of the Meiji Restoration, various contradictions have surfaced amidst the affluence. These include inflation, pollution, urban overcrowding, rural depopulation and stagnation, educational disorders, and the generation gap. Of all these problems, which are common to advanced countries, our lack of accumulated social overhead capital must be promptly rectified since it is now acting as a brake on national economic growth and the improvement of Japanese life.

Environmental pollution gets worse as industrial production grows. In 1968, industrial output in the Kanto Coastal Area centering on Tokyo was about $93 billion, discharging 550,000 tons of sulfur dioxide pollutants. According to forecasts by MITI (Ministry of International Trade and Industry), industrial output in the same region will reach $200 billion and the resulting discharge of sulfur dioxide pollutants will total 1,140,000 tons by 1975. If we accept the present pattern of industrial location, the problem of pollution will never be solved however much is invested in preventing pollution.

At the same time, improving urban living conditions and creating pleasant communities has become an urgent political task. If pollution controls are strengthened for such purposes, however, it may very conceivably constrain industrial activity in built-up areas. By the same token, the problems of rising prices cannot be solved simply by suppressing public utility charges and rationalizing the distribution system, because one of the main reasons for rising prices is the excessive concentration of population and industry in the urban areas. As industry expands, a total of 1,100 square miles will be needed as industrial sites by 1985, as against a total of 460 square miles in 1969. But in view of soaring land prices, it will be impossible for industry to secure these vast sites in already overcrowded areas. The demand for industrial water will increase from today's 90 million tons daily to an estimated 320 million tons. Yet it is difficult to locate water resources capable of supplying this industrial water along the developed Pacific coast.

If the present industrial structure of the Japanese economy remains unchanged, we will have to import 30 percent or more of the world's total trade in mineral and energy resources ten years hence. If this happens, super-tankers of the 500,000-ton dead-weight class will inevitably be introduced for efficient transportation, yet there are only four ports in all of Japan capable of handling such tankers: Shibushi Bay in Kagoshima Prefecture, Sukumo Bay in Kochi Prefecture, Tachibana Bay in Tokushima Prefecture, and Mutsu Bay in Aomori Prefecture. Thus revolutionary changes will be needed in our crude-oil import and transport procedures. Petroleum to be consumed in the Hanshin (Osaka-Kobe) area, for example, could be unloaded at Tachibana Bay. The three bridge routes between Shikoku Island and Honshu to be completed by 1985 thus will serve many purposes in that they may also carry pipelines for crude oil from Tachibana Bay to the Hanshin area and surplus water from the Yoshino River to industrial areas.

As many people may be expected to quit farming with the vigorous implementation of the Comprehensive Agricultural Policy, they must be given adequate opportunities to seek and find employment in secondary and tertiary industries near their homes. This was the thinking behind the enactment of the

Industrialization Promotion Law for Rural Districts. I do not subscribe to the small-time idea of simply bringing one factory to each village, but rather favor pump-priming by constructing big industrial infrastructures prior to the actual industrial relocation and bringing in core industries. Among the prospective coastal areas for such development are Kushiro, a second Tomakomai site, Mutsu-Ogawara, Coastal Akita, Nakaumi, Reclaimed Ariake Tideland, Shibushi Bay, Sukumo Bay, and Tachibana Bay.

Countermeasures for Overcrowding and Underpopulation

Thus, measures to deal with overcrowding and underpopulation are two sides of the same coin. My objective in the General Principles of Urban Policy was to solve both these problems simultaneously. The following four concrete policy measures have already been adopted within the philosophical framework of the General Principles:

1. The establishment of the Honshu-Shikoku Bridges Corporation;

2. The enactment of the National New Trunk Line Railroad Construction Law;

3. The promulgation of the Motor Vehicle Weight Tax Law;

4. Industrial relocation.

While the first two are generally accepted, the Motor Vehicle Weight Tax Law was severely criticized when I first proposed it, and people said I was crazy to try to tax cars and use the revenue to construct railway lines. Today, however, I hear little of such arguments or criticisms, and the concept seems to have been understood and accepted.

There were, admittedly, some deficiencies in our presentation of the automobile weight tax, but it always takes time for new taxes to be accepted. While many tax cuts have been carried out, the gasoline tax has been increased four or five times in the postwar period, and the gasoline tax may well be the only one that has been increased. Imposition of the motor vehicle weight tax was delayed until February 1, 1972, but the concerned parties have finally come to understand the need for such a levy.

The fourth concrete policy measure that has derived from "The General Principles of Urban Policy" was the initiation of industrial relocation. This was by no means an idea I simply happened to think of after being appointed Minister of International Trade and Industry, nor was it a fragmentary concept.

At present 73 percent of Japan's total industrial production is concentrated along the Pacific coast. To balance the archipelago, secondary industry must be distributed more evenly. We must try to induce manufacturing, the leading element in regional development, to be properly distributed in accordance with the development potential of each region. We want to move factories from areas of excessive industrial concentration to other areas and, at the same time, to locate new factories in underdeveloped regions, thus achieving industrial relocation on a national scale.

The first steps to implement this new policy were taken in 1972. The 68th Session of the Diet passed the Law for Promotion of Industrial Relocation and the Law Concerning Reforming the Coal Mining Area Development Association into the Industrial Relocation and Coal Mining Area Development Public Corporation, and $50 million was appropriated in the fiscal 1972 budget and in the Fiscal Investment and Loan Plan ($100 million on an annual basis). The taxation system is also to be revised accordingly. While none of these things will have an immediate policy impact, we will obviously reach an impasse unless someone does something. I hope this program will be fully understood, firmly established, and effectively used.

Keeping the Global Trends in Mind

My ideas for remodeling Japan will not be truly effective unless they are in harmony with the general trends in our rapidly changing world. The postwar Japanese economy has passed through the three stages of recovery, high growth, and internationalization. With the present open economy, we have effected full-fledged trade and capital liberalization, and in 1971 Japan boldly upvalued the yen as a part of the international currency realignment. This means that Japan has become accepted as an influential member of the international economic community both in name and reality. It reminds me of the time when I, as Minister of Finance, decided on the shift to Article VIII status within the IMF, and I am indeed overwhelmed at the tremendous progress we have made in our international position. If this giant Japanese economy is to develop further and to create a secure and prosperous life for its people, it is imperative above all else that world peace be preserved, especially in Asia, and that all members of the world community prosper under the principles of equality and reciprocity. In creating such a situation, Japan is now being asked to assume responsibilities commensurate with its real strength. Japan's foreign economic policy in the

Kakuei Tanaka, the author

Talking with U.S. President Nixon (*in Hawaii, August, 1972*)

Japan-U.S. summit talk in Hawaii,
normalizing relations with China, and. . .

—— to chart Japan's future

With China's Premier Chou En-lai (*in Peking, September, 1972*)

Addressing the Commission for Remodeling the Japanese Archipelago, comprising leaders in every field, with his Cabinet

People of Japan endorse "Remodeling"

photo: Konosuke Ishii
Tomihiro Kubota

Overcrowding and
underpopulation

— to get away
from the disequilibrium

Revamping the transport network

—— to solve congestion and to run bullet trains throughout the country

Shinjuku, one of Tokyo's subcenters

Urban redevelopment and a more peaceful life

Senri New Town, outside of Osaka

Kuzuryu Dam

To tap energy resources and to build academic towns ——

Institute for International Studies

photo: Nikkan Kogyo Shimbun, Ltd.

1970's will, therefore, have to be based upon positive action to establish:

1. Rules of trade under which countries at different stages of development may develop an internationally desirable division of labor for their mutual prosperity;

2. Rules of international investment to coordinate and harmonize the activities of multinational enterprises and the interests of each national economy;

3. Rules of conduct of aid-giving and aid-receiving nations conducive to the solution of the North-South problem;

4. An international monetary system and rules to permit smooth adjustment of disequilibriums in the balances of international payments and to solve the problems of insufficient liquidity and loss of confidence in key currencies.

The bipolar cold-war structure of the postwar world has basically thawed and the entire world is heading for an era of peaceful coexistence. On the other hand, the North-South problem has gotten worse. The postwar world order clearly faces an inevitable restructuring, both politically and economically. At this time of global change, Japan's domestic and foreign policy must undergo a fundamental review of its very premises. Japan's future course may be summarized in two words: peace and welfare. Externally, we must continue to uphold the principles of peace which we have consistently adhered to during the quartercentury following the last War and seek development in cooperation and friendship with the rest of the world. Internally, the traditional policy of giving top priority to industrial production and exports should be replaced by a policy for balanced economic growth promoting social overhead capital investment and improving social welfare to equal the standards of other advanced nations. It is to answer these challenges, both at home and abroad, that I have argued untiringly for a remodeling of the Japanese archipelago. I would like to devote myself to this great undertaking, making the best use of my twenty-five years of experience in the Diet, building a society which will be trusted by the entire world community, a society in which the Japanese people can be justly proud to be born, to work, and to die.

PART I

The Problems Facing Japan

1

Remodeling the Nation

Forces that Built Modern Japan

It was in June, 1859, nine years before the Meiji Restoration, that Japan made the crucial decision to open the country triggered by Commodore Perry's visit to Japan. In the preceding two hundred and twenty-odd years, the Tokugawa Shogunate had kept the country closed to foreign influence. This opening of the country was the point when modern industry was introduced and fostered.

Along with various measures to enrich, strengthen, and enlighten the country, the Meiji Government undertook to promote capitalism by developing industry in order to preserve Japan's independence and effect its rapid modernization. In the beginning, the priority was on light industries. Modern silk mills were constructed in Tomioka (Gunma Prefecture) under government management. Sakai (Osaka Prefecture) was the location selected for government-run cotton mills. These pioneering factories were all located within easy access of raw materials and labor. In the area of the heavy and chemical industries, which were strengthened during the period between the Russo-Japanese War and World War I, Yawata (Fukuoka Prefecture) and Muroran (Hokkaido) were selected as ideal sites for steel mills because of their proximity to coal sources. These were then surrounded by related mechanized factories. Copper smelting works were also built at Niihama in the vicinity of the Besshi Copper Mines (Ehime Prefecture). This location pattern was based upon the same reasoning as the earlier location of the silk and cotton industries.

After World War I, however, a new approach to industrial location was advanced. Instead of dispersing factories so as to be convenient to raw material sources, the new pattern was to concentrate factories in order to create industrial zones. A representative example of this new trend is the Keihin (Tokyo and Yokohama) industrial zone running all the way from Tokyo to Yokohama. Mr. Soichiro Asano established the Tsurumi Reclamation Company in 1912 and reclaimed two square miles of land for industrial purposes along the Tsurumi Coast. This was a radical departure from the traditional approach to plant location, as this site was not close to raw material resources. It was most favorably situated with a port convenient for the transportation of raw materials and finished goods, with the major consumer market of Tokyo behind it, and suitable also to modern industry's tendency to seek economies by large concentrations.

By around 1935, the four big industrial zones of the prewar period had been completed in the Hanshin (Osaka-Kobe), Chukyo (Nagoya and vicinity), Kita-Kyushu (northern Kyushu),

Employment Trends By Industry

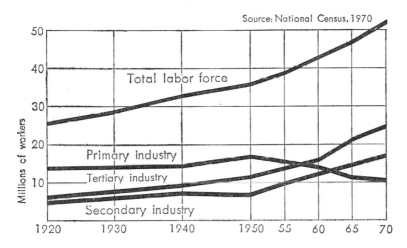

Source: National Census, 1970

and Keihin (Tokyo-Yokohama) areas, all built at approximately the same time.

Industrial development and the formation of the industrial zones inevitably brought about concentrations of population and tertiary industries such as commerce and services, causing rapid urbanization at the same time. From then on, the concentration of population and industry in urban centers continued unabated until well into World War II. This industrial development, of course, resulted in the growth of Japan's GNP and national income.

I find that the following basic propositions can be derived from this brief economic history of Japan. One is that GNP and national income increase in inverse proportion to the percentage of the labor force employed in primary industries as well as in direct proportion to increasing urbanization. For example, the share of the labor force employed in primary

29

industries, 90 percent in 1868, was down to 54 percent in 1920, 44 percent in 1930, and 17.4 percent in 1970. As the percentage of the labor force engaging in primary industries declined and as the other sectors' shares consequently increased, Japan's GNP and national income have increased.

The next proposition is that GNP and national income increase in proportion to the expansion of the individual's radius of mobility within one day. People used to travel from Tokyo to Osaka on foot. Even when trains became available about the middle of the Meiji Era, it still was a twenty-hour trip. Now we have expressways, the New Tokaido Line, and jet aircraft to make the trip from Tokyo to Osaka in a matter of hours. The greater the one-day travel distance, the greater the economic expansion. One might even conclude, therefore, that the gross output and income of all mankind will increase in proportion with increased mobility. In this way, industry has developed, pursuing the economies and advantages of concentration, which in turn served to strengthen the nation and its economy.

Postwar Economy: From Rags to Riches

The concentration of industry and population in urban areas was further accelerated by the postwar economic growth.

Japan's postwar economy expanded in three stages— recovery, rapid growth, and internationalization. These three stages may also be designated as those of quantitative expansion, qualitative improvement, and then excellence by international standards. Another way of phrasing these stages might be as the eras of food, clothing, and shelter.

On August 15, 1945, Japan unconditionally accepted the Potsdam Declaration which ended World War II. This war had annihilated the Japanese economy. Forty-four percent of Japan's total prewar territory was lost, and industrial and mining production was down from 1935–1937 levels to only 30 percent for consumer goods and 10 percent for capital goods. During the quarter of a century since then, we have achieved an economic growth described as a "miracle" in building today's prosperity. Who could have foreseen today's Japan at the War's end?

For some years after the War, we wore rags, had empty stomachs, and lived a hand-to-mouth existence while struggling with economic recovery. Former munitions factories eked out a living by producing pots and pans, hoes and spades.

The adoption of the priority production system and American aid helped the economy to get back on its feet. The P.P.S. was put into effect in January, 1947, to give special priority to the production of key industrial materials such as coal, iron, and steel. To end the inflation and to reestablish the market economy, a uniform exchange rate of ¥360 to the dollar was set in 1949 and a tightly balanced budget was achieved. The economy had to be rationalized whatever the cost, and, as a result, enterprises returned to the principles of good management, e.g., efficiency, cost, productivity, and profit, which had been forsaken during the long years of war.

Although inflation was controlled, exports failed to grow because of the weak world market and increased inventories. Effective domestic demand declined owing to tougher tax laws. The result was recession.

The start of the Korean Conflict in June, 1950, however, brought about a radical change in economic conditions both at home and abroad. The sudden increase in exports and procurements by the U.S. Armed Forces spurred the Japanese economy to rising production and modernization. Production levels rose to equal and even to surpass prewar levels as early as October that same year. In August, 1952, Japan was admitted to membership in the International Monetary Fund, which had been established to facilitate stable exchange rates and more liberal foreign-exchange markets. As an IMF Article XIV status member, Japan took its first steps toward international acceptance, marking the completion of the postwar period of economic recovery.

Reviewing economic development between 1945 and 1955 from the standpoint of industrial location, industry first recovered and raised production levels in the four existing industrial zones. Around the time of the Korean Conflict, new industrial sites were sought. The oil industry, for example, located its refineries near consumer centers in former Imperial Navy oil depots, such as Yokkaichi in Mie Prefecture and Iwakuni and Tokuyama in Yamaguchi Prefecture. In the iron and steel industry, President Yataro Nishiyama of Kawasaki Steel Co. came up with the idea in 1950 of reclaiming the coast of Chiba and building an integrated steel works there. This then attracted other industries and grew to be today's Keiyo (Tokyo-Chiba) industrial zone.

The following decade between 1955 and 1965 was the era of rapid growth. Spurred by the world-wide boom, Japan's exports rose and, coupled with good agricultural harvests, we enjoyed "growth without inflation" and "quantitative boom." Production in the mining and manufacturing industries rose to about twice 1934–1936 levels and surpassed the record prewar figures of 1944. I recall even now how *The 1956 Economic White Paper* noted that "the postwar era is over."

32

The next decade, 1955–1965, was one of rapid growth, supported by the emergence of new goods and new industries which were based upon private plant and equipment investment and technical innovation. The result was rapid development in the heavy and chemical industries as they came to account for 62.8 percent of all production by 1961. Japan was now a heavy-and-chemical-industry economy along with the U.S. and U.S.S.R. The era of mass consumption centering around mass sales of household electrical appliances also arrived, and in 1960 the Ikeda Cabinet unveiled its national income doubling plan, which further stimulated economic growth.

Throughout this period, the dramatic shift from coal to petroleum as the principal energy source, increasing dependence upon imports of raw materials, and the needs of the mass-consumption market facilitated the construction of major industrial complexes for electric power, iron and steel, ship-building, chemicals, and petroleum refining in or near the big cities along the Pacific coast. These industrial concentrations also attracted financial, commercial, and service activities to these areas.

As if it had been waiting for Japan's rapid economic growth, the IMF Board of Executive Directors recommended in February, 1963, that Japan should assume the obligation of Article VIII, on the grounds that "Japan no longer qualifies for continued exchange restrictions on imports and other current transactions for balance-of-payments reasons." Accepting this recommendation, Japan took on Article VIII status in April of the next year. At about this time, Japan was also accepted for membership in the Organization for Economic Co-operation and Development (OECD), an organization founded upon the principle of liberalizing capital transactions. Thus Japan joined the advanced international community both in name and in fact, and was ready to embark with an open economy into the rough international seas.

In June of 1967, Japan decided upon the basic principles of liberalization of capital transactions, and in July Phase One of this liberalization program was implemented. After two more phases of liberalization, the fourth or final round was put into effect in August, 1971.

In contrast to the decade of rapid economic growth, the new Sato Government, taking the administrative reins in November, 1964, announced stable growth as its economic objective. Nevertheless, during the 1965–1970 period, sales of such products as color television sets and automobiles led the economy to a growth rate of more than 10 percent. The heavy and chemical industries also grew proportionately to enhance the economy's international competitiveness. In 1968, Japan's balance of international payments became favorable, eliminating balance-of-payments considerations as a restrictive factor to further expansion. As the years went by, this surplus grew to bring Japan's foreign-exchange reserves to $4.4 billion as of the end of 1970, $7.9 billion as of July, 1971, and $14.8 billion as of November of the same year. Finally, in December, the yen was revalued upward by 16.88 percent to a rate of ¥308 to the dollar as part of the multilateral international currency realignment. During all this time, the postwar Japanese economy continued to average a real rate of growth of 10 percent.

However, the rapid economic development since 1965 only further aggravated the urban concentration of industry and population, and the disadvantages of urban overcrowding and rural depopulation began to become pronounced.

Rural Exodus and Urban Concentration

If you place the compass needle at the very center of Tokyo (Nihonbashi) and draw a circle with a radius of 30 miles, this circle will encompass cities such as Chigasaki in Kanagawa Prefecture and Ryugasaki in Ibaraki Prefecture. Doing the same for Osaka and Nagoya, taking Osaka Station and Nagoya Station as their centers, the Osaka circle includes Akashi in Hyogo Prefecture and Otsu in Shiga Prefecture, while Nagoya's circle includes Sekigahara in Gifu Prefecture and Gamagoori in Aichi Prefecture.

According to the 1970 census, 33 million people live within 30 miles of the centers of Japan's three largest cities. This means that 32 percent of the total population lives on one percent of the land. Japan has a total area smaller than the single state of California, and a population as large as Spain's living on less than one percent of the land. Small wonder there are problems.

Of these three urban centers, the nation's capital city of Tokyo is remarkably overcrowded. Here 11,410,000 people, 11 percent of the total population, live on six-tenths of one percent of the land. To better understand how very overcrowded Tokyo is, consider that an additional 1,900,000 commute into central Tokyo every day. These people come from outlying areas around Tokyo (Kanagawa, Saitama, and Chiba Prefectures) for work or study.

Extraordinary traffic congestion is a vivid symbol of the overcrowded situation. During the rush hours, the National Railway's commuter lines in Tokyo carry 276 percent of prescribed capacity between Ueno and Okachimachi, 265 percent between

35

Mikawashima and Nippori, and 256 percent between Hirai and Kameido. Most trunk railway lines handle more than two-and-a-half times their prescribed capacities. To illustrate these figures, 250 percent of capacity represents a situation where physical movement is impossible, and at 300 percent of capacity breathing becomes difficult and the crush can prove to be physically dangerous.

Besides Tokyo itself, the entire National Capital Sphere is also notable for its excessive concentration of population. The National Capital Sphere embraces Tokyo and the seven prefectures surrounding Tokyo (Kanagawa, Yamanashi, Saitama, Chiba, Tochigi, Ibaraki, and Gunma). The population of this area in 1970 was 30,260,000, an increase of 3,290,000 during the preceding five years alone.

The massive inflow of young people to the National Capital Sphere has also generated a big difference in birth rates between the Capital and Kinki (centering on Osaka) Spheres and the rural districts. Even if the population flow were to stop now, the big urban centers contain most of the young people who will be ready for work or marriage in ten to fifteen years.

As a part of this process, a new phenomenon, that of population drain from centers of big urban areas, has also received considerable attention. This may seem at first glance to contradict the ever-growing concentration of population in the National Capital Sphere but does not. Rather, it should be seen as the end product of overcrowding. Soaring land prices in the twenty-three wards of central Tokyo pose grave difficulties for new housing construction. The environmental disruption caused by Tokyo's more than 2,300,000 cars has deteriorated living conditions in the city.

Tokyo's three central wards of Chiyoda, Chuo, and Minato have been losing population since around 1955, while the five adjacent wards of Shinjuku, Shibuya, Toshima, Taito, and Bunkyo followed suit within a few years. In 1965, Shinagawa, Meguro, and Ōta wards also felt the effects of this population exodus.

The accompanying phenomenon is an advancing urban sprawl as people fleeing central Tokyo have been pouring into the three surrounding prefectures of Chiba, Kanagawa, and Saitama in a disordered jumble of housing development. As long as this trend continues, the National Capital Sphere's population in 1985 will increase by ten million to reach a level of more than forty million people.

Tokyo's Cherry Blossoms Are Dying

Until very recently mankind has been living in a natural cycle, obtaining materials from nature, processing and consuming them, and discharging them as waste but within nature's self-cleansing capabilities, thus maintaining a natural balance. We Japanese were no exception. But in the process of our rapid economic growth starting around 1955, the urban concentrations of population and industry have exceeded natural purification capabilities, creating grave problems of environmental pollution.

Big urban areas have come to suffer from sulfur dioxide from automobile exhaust and factory smoke. Water pollution in rivers and seas is becoming more serious as industrial effluent and residential sewage go untreated for lack of adequate sewage systems. Heavy metals such as mercury and cadmium have polluted fish and farm products. These phenomena have been condemned as undermining our health and destroying our life, and there has been an increasing public outcry calling for their solution. More recently, plastic containers and discarded household durables such as refrigerators and television sets have created new social problems because of the disposal difficulties which they pose.

Let us look more closely at air and water pollution.

According to an air pollution survey carried out by the Ministry of International Trade and Industry in areas facing the Bay of Tokyo, the amount of sulfur dioxides generated during 1968 totaled 605,000 tons in sulfur equivalent. Of this, 55,000 tons were treated, but the remaining 550,000 tons of sulfur dioxides were discharged, causing pollution controversy. Only 9 percent of these effluents are treated.

If the present pattern of industrial location is allowed to continue, even with sulfur recovery equipment and a higher treatment ratio, the aggregate of pollutants discharged in areas around the Bay of Tokyo in 1975 will be twice today's. The total amount of sulfur dioxides will reach 1,440,000 tons, and even a treatment ratio of 21 percent will discharge 1,130,000 tons into the air. This is an increase of 207 percent over the 1968 level.

Close observation of cherry (*Prunus yedoensis*) trees in Tokyo also shows the clear effects of air pollution; the petals on these trees are thinner, the colors more faded, and the leaves smaller than on trees in less urbanized areas. In several years, unless something is done, there may be no more cherry blossoms in Tokyo. Also, even allowing for man's adaptability to a changing environment, respiratory illnesses such as chronic bronchitis,

38

and a resultant rise in the death rate, will be unavoidable under conditions of such severe air pollution.

With water pollution, things are just as bad. According to a joint survey carried out by Tokyo, Saitama Prefecture, Chiba Prefecture, and Kanagawa Prefecture, major rivers in the area, such as the Edo River, Arakawa River, and Tama River, all suffer from far higher levels of pollution than the state ecological standards. In the case of the Edo River, approximately 11 tons of pollutants daily (measured in terms of Biological Oxygen Demand) flow in at the Kuriyama Gate. Water in the Edo River has a BOD level of 2.1 to 3 ppm upstream from the Nagareyama Bridge (which is about 15 miles from the river mouth), and 3.1 to 5 ppm further upstream at the Kuriyama Gate. Water polluted to such an extent is fit only for agricultural purposes. In order to make the water upstream from the Kuriyama Gate clean enough to satisfy national standards, the BOD pollutant level in the water flowing in should be lowered to a maximum of three tons per day. This would mean a reduction of 70 percent.

Air and water in urban areas are becoming dirtier every day. Unless something is done and done soon, they will constitute a danger to the health of our citizens.

This danger is illustrated by a Ministry of Home Affairs survey which revealed that, out of 40,854 complaints about pollution that were filed in fiscal 1969, 70 percent of these came from the industrial centers of Tokyo, Osaka, and Nagoya.

Crisis in Power Supply

For some years now, there has been a fear of electric power

shortage during the summer, when demand peaks, and the utility companies have been seriously contemplating countermeasures. The peak period of power demand used to be December, but this has now changed to August. This is both because of the nationwide increase in household air-conditioning and because of a sharp increase in air-conditioning in large commercial facilities. Power companies are asking their institutional customers to adjust their power consumption through such means as staggered holidays during the summer. But if there is a serious drought or major breakdown in the big power plants, power could be cut off with little or no notice.

The Kasumigaseki Building is Japan's first true skyscraper, boasting some thirty-six floors. This building alone consumes 29 million kwh of electricity per year, or the equivalent of 16,000 households. And skyscraper construction is booming in Tokyo, Osaka and Nagoya.

As a precaution, the Kansai Electric Company asked its major customers to stagger their holidays from July 13 to September 10, 1971. This stop-gap effort called for the users to operate plants on Sundays when the load is relatively low and to close down on a weekday instead.

But this created new problems. One meat-processing plant had a large number of part-time employees who were also housewives, and many of them did not show up on Sunday. Others complained of working Sundays because they could not secure commuter bus service. Obviously, this measure does not provide a lasting solution.

As for fiscal 1972, we expect to have an average excess capacity of 8 percent nationwide. This is due to slack industrial demand owing to the recession, and does not in any way signal a long-range turn for the better.

According to a long-term forecast on power supply and demand issued by the Japan Electric Power Survey Committee in February, 1972, the 1976 total demand for power will be 570.5 billion kwh, about 1.8 times the 1970 figure. This same forecast also predicts an average annual increase in power demand of about 10 percent, and a summer peak demand of up to 94,610,000 kw (twice 1970's). In order for this demand to be met, it will be necessary to allow all the development plans of the power companies to be faithfully executed.

These power resource development plans call for supplying an additional 105,890,000 kw by the end of 1980, broken down into 13,530,000 kw hydro, 59,460,000 kw thermal, and 39,900,-000 kw nuclear. But there are already six projects with a total output of 5,820,000 kw that have been granted permission for construction by the Electric Power Development Coordinating Council, but on which construction has not yet begun. These include Kansai Electric's Nos. 1 and 2 Thermal Plants at Shin-miyazu, the Nos. 1 and 2 Nuclear Plants at Omeshi, and others. Of the projects which were to be started in fiscal 1971 to provide an additional 20 million kw, the final plans for only 14,160,000 kw have been approved.

The delays are caused by opposition to these projects by local residents, in the case of thermal power generators, on the grounds that the sulfur dioxide emissions from burning heavy oil will pollute the air and the warm water discharges will adversely affect fishing in the area. In the case of atomic power plants, there are also strong apprehensions about the danger of radioactivity, fears of environmental pollution, and opposition by fishermen who fear their fishing grounds will be ruined by warm water discharges. Unless these problems are solved, it will indeed be difficult to resolve the tight power situation.

A Six-Mile-an-Hour Motor Society

As Japan's economic growth continues with rising income levels and increasing spare time, automobile transport has grown dramatically, greatly extending the people's radius of mobility. The mode of life has changed to one based on "door to door" transportation, and the new "motorized society" has appeared.

In the case of Japan, however, the popularity of automobiles is more recent than in America and Europe, but the pace of motorization has been extremely fast. As a result, road construction and maintenance have not kept up with the increasing numbers of cars.

Ever since the first Five-Year Plan for Road Improvement was set forth in 1954, and especially during the last few years, road improvements have been carried out vigorously. To look at expressways alone, the Meishin Expressway between Komaki (Aichi Prefecture) and Nishinomiya (Hyogo Prefecture), totaling 120 miles, was completed in 1963. This was followed by the 215-mile Tomei Expressway from Tokyo to Komaki and the 55-mile Fujiyoshida (Shizuoka Prefecture) section of the Chuo Expressway between Chofu (Tokyo) and Fujiyoshida.

Among those planned for completion in 1972 or 1973 are the 60-mile Tohoku Throughway between Iwatsuki and Utsunomiya, the 15-mile Kyushu Throughway from Minamiseki to Ueki, the 5-mile Chuo Expressway from Takaido to Chofu, and the 15-mile Hokuriku Expressway from Kanazawa to Komatsu (Ishikawa Prefecture). By fiscal 1974, a total of 1,200 miles of expressways will be completed, and by fiscal 1985 the total length will be 4,700 miles.

Expenditures for road construction in fiscal 1972 will be $7.2 billion, a 2.7-fold jump over fiscal 1965. But as of February, 1972, automobile ownership was up to 21,100,000 vehicles (2,350,000 of them in Tokyo), an increase of 2.4 times since 1965. Thus we have a vicious cycle with increasing road construction barely keeping up with automobile ownership.

Road construction is unable to get ahead of the increase in the number of cars because of the annual rise in construction costs. For instance, the second phase of the Tokyo Metropolitan Expressway No. 3 cost $10,000 per yard, and the Ikeda Line of the Hanshin Expressway cost $9,000 per yard. When compared with the cost of the Meishin Expressway ($2,000) and the Tomei Expressway ($3,300), it is clear how much costs have risen.

Japan also has a very low percentage of paved roads. Compared to Great Britain's 100 percent, Italy's 88.8 percent, France's 82.6 percent, West Germany's 76.7 percent, and the U.S.'s 43.7 percent, the corresponding figure for Japan is a low 12.7 percent, ranking it 57th in the world and certainly lowest among the advanced nations.

Such conditions have made traffic jams and traffic accidents a daily routine, and have created a major social issue, what we call "traffic wars." Especially in such crowded areas as Tokyo, Osaka, and Nagoya, traffic congestion is worsening day by day, even to the extent of seriously hindering everyday work and general economic activity. This is because Japan's urban road ratio (the percentage of total city area used as streets) is strikingly low in comparison with the main cities in the U.S. and Europe. The percentage ratios are 43 percent for Washington D.C., 35 percent for New York, 25 percent for Paris, 23 percent for London, 12 percent for Tokyo, 18 percent for Nagoya, and only 9 percent for Osaka.

Because of these and other reasons, the costs of collecting and distributing goods by truck have risen steadily. According to a survey by the Japan Transport Economics Research Center, Tokyo's major trucking companies' collection and delivery costs for one ton of goods, $3.06 in 1959, rose by 16 percent to $3.55 by 1963 and by 67 percent to $5.90 in 1969. More recent figures would surely be still higher.

Traffic congestion in the big cities is unbearable, and automobile speed has been reduced significantly. A survey by the Kanto Area Construction Bureau in the fall of 1971 reported that the average speed of automobiles on the 125 miles of national roads within Tokyo was 12.5 miles per hour—and that this was down to 5.6 miles per hour during the morning and evening rush hours. Another survey, this one by the Tokyo Metropolitan Government in 1971, showed average speeds on Route 6 from Nihonbashi through Sudacho and Ueno to Asakusa and on Route 17 from Nihonbashi through Hitotsubashi and Jimbo-cho to Sugamo of 2.5 miles per hour and 4.8 miles per hour respectively. We can do better on foot over a short distance.

As of February, 1972, there were 21,100,000 privately owned automobiles in Japan, the second largest number in the world. But by 1985 the number will be nearly doubled to 40 million. In December, 1970, the length of paved road per automobile was a mere 25 feet. This was less than one-third of the U.S. and British figures, and about one-sixth the French figure. Unless we make an all-out effort to construct more roads and to raise the pavement ratio, each and every road in Japan may be flooded

Motor Vehicle Ownership Growth

Millions of vehicles

Year	5	10	15	20
1966	●●●●●	●●●(		
1967	●●●●●	●●●●(		
1968	●●●●●	●●●●●	●(	
1969	●●●●●	●●●●●	●●●●	
1970	●●●●●	●●●●●	●●●●●	●(
1971	●●●●●	●●●●●	●●●●●	●●●(
1972 (Feb.)	●●●●●	●●●●●	●●●●●	●●●●● ●

Source: 1971 Statistical Handbook of Japan's Transport Economics

The Percentage of Paved Roads

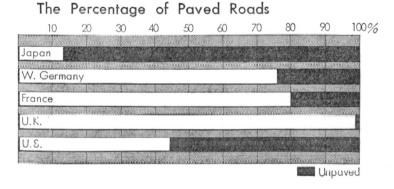

■ Unpaved

with immobilized automobiles. Even now, many car owners do not drive their cars but only display them because of the difficulties and dangers of driving in Tokyo. They claim that it is not the act of driving but the mere possession of an automobile which is significant. This is not sarcasm. It is reality attesting to the gravity of the situation.

With a greater number of cars, the costs of road maintenance soar very rapidly. At present, road maintenance costs per automobile amount to $1,700 per person on national average. But the corresponding figure is estimated to be $51,000 in Tokyo. These are all staggering figures, but I want you to know that they are all factual.

Dearth of Parks

In April, 1971, Dr. Ryokichi Minobe won the Governorship of Tokyo, campaigning on a platform of "blue skies and open spaces for Tokyoites." As the Secretary General of the Liberal Democratic Party at the time, I led the losing campaign, which drove home to me anew how deeply the metropolitan residents long for "blue skies and open spaces."

According to a survey conducted by the Ministry of Construction in 1971, buildings in the seven central wards of Chiyoda, Chuo, Minato, Shinagawa, Shibuya, Shinjuku, and Bunkyo average two stories, but the corresponding figure for the rest of Tokyo's twenty-three wards is 1.7. Low-rise buildings are squeezed together endlessly in all directions, and Tokyo has only little bits and pieces of parks and playgrounds for its children.

Growing children must play on the steps of apartment houses or dodge cars in the back streets. In a school composition, one boy described how he was scolded by a policeman for being away from home so early in the morning when he had gone by train to claim a place for his baseball team on a dry river bed some distance away. In an accurate summation of Tokyo's plight, Kenzo Mizoguchi has written in his book *Frontiers in Education: Children in the Midst of Overpopulation and Underpopulation:* "There have been cases in which children taken

46

out to wide open spaces to play and romp only looked puzzled and finally sat down on the grass to play cards."

Guidelines established for urban parks in Japan stipulate that 65 square feet of park should be available for each resident. In Tokyo, however, there were only 13 square feet of space for each resident as of the end of 1971, as little as one-fifth of its set standard. Parks have an important role to play in the urban setting. Citizens look to them as places for elderly citizens to enjoy the sunshine, mothers to tend their children, and lovers to enjoy each other's company. Parks are also places of refuge in times of natural disaster. They help us to revitalize our humanity and are citadels for protecting life.

How many parks are there in Tokyo then? In March, 1971, the Ministry of Construction reported that there were 1,958 parks in the twenty-three wards, 571 parks in suburban cities, and 31 parks in outlying areas, altogether 2,560 parks covering 3,500 acres. This is one-tenth of New York's total park area (37,000 acres) and less than onehalf of that of Paris (7,400 acres).

Tokyo's model park, Hibiya Park, has an area of less than 40 acres, while Central Park in New York covers an areas of 840 acres, more than twenty times bigger than Hibiya. As compared to the 13 square feet of park for each Tokyo citizen, New Yorkers have 207 square feet, Londoners 245 square feet, and Berliners 266 square feet.

Walking in the Luxembourg Gardens in Paris, one sees people only here and there with birds singing and squirrels running about. It hardly ever happens that there are swarms of people occupying all the benches with no space left over to sit down, as on holidays in Japan. This in itself is eloquent proof that the importance of parks and greens is better understood abroad.

Anti-Earthquake Measures Imperative

Downtown Tokyo is full of wooden one- or two-story houses. What would a big earthquake or a fire do in such an area? On September 1, 1923, the Great Kanto Earthquake struck Tokyo. This quake had a magnitude of 7.9 on the Richter scale in Tokyo with an intensity of 6 ("violent") on the Japanese scale of 7. According to existing records, the calamitous fires that broke out burned for forty hours over a period of three days and nights, and claimed about 60,000 lives. If the missing are included, well over 100,000 people fell victim. All 38,000 who sought shelter at the Army's Clothes Depot in Tokyo were burned to death in this living hellfire. The total damage was over $33 million, which would be several billion dollars at current prices.

What if an earthquake of the same scale as the Kanto Earthquake struck Tokyo today? According to the Metropolitan Disaster Prevention Council and the Metropolitan Fire Board, it would destroy 20,000 homes, crush 2,000 people to death, and burn a total of 6 square miles (equivalent to Shinagawa and Nakano wards combined), burning an estimated 560,000 people to death within five hours. This is indeed a horrifying possibility. It is estimated that 80 percent of the downtown wards of Sumida, Katsushika, Edogawa, and Koto would be burned down within five hours because of their heavy concentrations of wooden houses.

From the standpoint of disaster prevention, conditions are worse now than they were in 1923, with the heavier residential crowding, the proliferation of such dangerous objects as petroleum and chemical products, a far greater number of

48

automobiles, and the numerous underground shopping centers.

As of March, 1971, Tokyo's twenty-three wards had 2,500 gasoline stations which they did not have at the time of the Kanto Earthquake, and these are natural combustion points.

The increase in the number of automobiles defies comparison. In 1923, there were only 4,400 automobiles. Today there are 2,350,000 (as of February, 1972). Needless to say, each of these is a potential fire-hazard.

Skyscrapers and other tall buildings pose yet another problem. In the evening of May 13, 1972, a fire broke out at the seven-story Sennichi Department Store building in Osaka and killed one hundred and eighteen people. The Osaka Fire Department mobilized fifty-two fire engines, ladder trucks, and aerial operation units to control the fire, but even so, many people jumped to their deaths. This building was 73 feet high, but the seven ladder trucks, including some which could reach 103 feet, were not able to rescue all the people on the roof. And this is just one isolated fire.

As of March, 1972, the Tokyo Fire Department had thirty-one ladder trucks, eight aerial operation units, and three seven-seated helicopters. Thus the Metropolitan Fire Board is not being alarmist when it says, "If a second Kanto Earthquake should strike today, the only thing we could do is to let it burn itself out."

The construction of underground shopping centers and arcades also constitutes a big problem. By the end of March, 1972, there were some eighty-eight underground shopping centers in Tokyo, including the 7.2 acre Shinjuku Station Underground Development. There is no need to describe the consequences of a big fire here.

A major earthquake would cause a great many of these disaster points to go up all at once, and the cumulative effect would be to create uncontrollable confusion.

From the standpoint of industry too, the Kanto area produces 37 percent of the nation's total industrial output, and a direct blow to these industrial facilities would shake the economy to its very foundations.

Livelihood Threatened by Spiraling Prices

According to the Statistics Bureau of the Prime Minister's Office, the 1965 consumer price index had risen 30.4 percent by 1970 and 38.3 percent by 1971. Price increases for consumer goods are especially noteworthy in the big cities. As of 1970, the price level in the seven biggest cities in the country, including Tokyo and Osaka, was 11.1 percent higher than in rural areas. One major reason for this discrepancy is the soaring prices of perishables such as fish and vegetables.

A survey carried out by the Tokyo Metropolitan Government reveals that a total of 901,000 tons of vegetables were brought into Tokyo in 1958; by 1970 this increased 75 percent to 1,587,-000 tons. During the same period, there was a nearly 65 percent increase in the amount of fish brought in, from 502,000 tons to 826,000 tons. Even so, the 1970 price indices (1965 = 100) were 139.3 for vegetables and 178.8 for fish.

The Central Wholesale Market made a survey and reported that saurel, a popular fish, cost 45 cents per pound in April, 1966, and $1.40 in April, 1972. The price of squid also rose from 60 cents to $1.80 during the same period. Such rapid price increases are due in part to the supply-and-demand imbalance caused by the population increase in Tokyo, but more directly to the outdated, irrational distribution system which passes on the increasing handling and payroll costs to consumers.

The Japan Real Estate Institute reports that the price of land in the six largest cities (Tokyo, Osaka, Nagoya, etc.) jumped from an index base of 100 in March, 1955, to 1,965 in March, 1971, an almost twenty-fold increase in fifteen years. This was due to the excessive concentration of population and industry in these six cities during the period of high economic growth (the decade or so following 1955) and the consequent rapid increase in demand for the limited land resources.

White collar workers labor diligently until retirement when they receive a lump-sum retirement allowance averaging $13,000 to $17,000. Yet even at retirement, they are more than likely not able to fulfill their life-long dream of owning a house and lot of their own, even if they are willing to settle for a site two to three hours' train ride from central Tokyo.

Poverty of Housing

More than one million new houses were constructed in Japan in fiscal 1965. Since then an annual increase of more than 10 percent has been maintained. As a result, the total number of houses and apartment units, including both private and public construction, was 28,650,000 as of the end of December, 1970.

In spite of this quantitative increase in housing facilities the housing shortage in urban centers is far from solved. Especially in big cities and their suburbs, the inflow of population surpasses the speed of construction, making the housing problem still more acute. In terms of floor space per person, the 1968 national average was 100 square feet. In Tokyo the average was 80 square feet and in Osaka 82 square feet, according to a survey by the Prime Minister's Office. These figures include dining rooms, kitchens, and other family space, so available private space is even less.

Tokyo has a far greater number of people renting houses or rooms than other areas. As of July, 1968, 1,292,000, or 42 percent of the total of 2,970,000 housing units were being rented. Of these rented housing units, nearly 70 percent, or 819,000, are wooden apartments. The average space per household in privately leased houses is 153 square feet, and in the wooden apartments it is only 116 square feet. Subtracting the space necessary for furniture and appliances, this leaves barely enough space to sleep. The vast majority use common dining facilities and toilets, making the living conditions extremely poor. Such conditions are not at all appropriate to the healthy and pleasant life our people seek, not to mention the cultural life.

Mr. Takeshi Nakamura, a novelist and former President of the Tokyo Lodgers' Association, writes that "urban Japanese are destined to live the life of a lodger in a privately operated apartment at least once, and the period of such lodging is becoming longer and longer." Many people come to the Association for help, complaining of high contract renewal charges or of clauses specifying that they must vacate if they have children, which shows how unstable the renter's life is.

If the renter is lucky, he will be admitted, against heavy odds, to a public apartment. This apartment, two rooms plus a dining-kitchen, rents for about $65 a month and is located one or two hours away from downtown Tokyo by rush-hour train. Even when, after innumerable difficulties, he begins earning enough to own a house, spiraling land prices automatically eliminate downtown Tokyo from consideration. Land selling at $10 per square foot can only be found outside the 25-mile radius, two hours from Tokyo. If he wants a site one-and-a-half hours from downtown Tokyo, the site alone costs well over that figure. Construction costs are also rising these days, and it will be difficult for him to build anything for under $10 per square foot even after he buys the land.

What are the chances of buying into a public development in central Tokyo then? If it has three rooms with a combination dining room, living room, and kitchen, it will cost $23,000. Even here, there are more than seven hundred applicants for every opening because even this is more advantageous than buying land and building a house on one's own. The fact is that it is practically impossible for people living in urban areas to obtain low-cost, pleasant housing

U-Turn Workers

One big company in Osaka scours the rural areas in search of youths who wish to go to work after they finish the nine years of compulsory education. This company even sends each potential employee a gift of an electric washing machine when he or she is in the seventh grade and a vacuum cleaner in the eighth grade in order to please the parents and make certain that the youth will come to work for the firm. We say of our employers' hiring practice that they "buy rice while it is still green in the paddy." But this is more like "buying rice seeds." Another big company, this time in Tokyo, spends $1,300 to secure one young worker just out of junior high school. But since half of these boys and girls leave their first jobs fairly soon in search of other work, the actual costs of securing each employee are, in effect, said to be double the surface figures.

A survey by the Prime Minister's Office reveals that in fiscal 1970 there were 17,550,000 young people in their teens and twenties in the labor market. But this number will decline by as many as 1,340,000, to 16,210,000 in fiscal 1975. The growth rate of the entire labor force is also slowing as it reflects a slower population growth. Japan's labor population increased an average of 820,000 people each year from 1963 to 1967, but the corresponding figure dropped to 570,000 annually from 1967 to 1970.

Labor market conditions are characterized by a lack of labor in factories located in big cities, where there is a conspicuous shortage of skilled labor, as the incoming workers generally prefer office and service work to blue-collar jobs.

I specifically want to point out the recent "U-turn" phenomenon occurring among young workers. For example, Kagoshima Prefecture reports that 44,700 young people moved out in search of job opportunities during 1970 alone, but that 3,500 of them came back to Kagoshima during that same year. More than 60 percent of the returning workers are twenty-five years of age or younger, and most of them have put down roots. They explain their return by citing the "lower salary but better life," "good environment," and "fuller use made of their skills."

Breakdown of Rural Community Life

In striking contrast to the overcrowded situation in the urban centers, local communities in outlying areas have been steadily losing population, creating a major social problem. The national census of 1970 revealed that a total of twenty-two prefectures lost population in the decade of the 1960's (six of the seven prefectures in Kyushu, five prefectures in the Tohoku area all four prefectures in Shikoku, three prefectures in the Chugoku area, and two prefectures each for Hokuriku and Kanto). Between 1965 and 1970, 2,345, or 70 percent of all cities, towns, and villages, lost population.

As heavy and chemical industries developed, accompanied by nationwide urbanization after 1955, people in rural areas left their homes for the better paying jobs, and the young people rushed to the bright lights of the cities.

Yamada City in Fukuoka Prefecture was a prosperous mining town with a population of 30,140 in 1960. But when the mines were closed due to the conversion from coal to petroleum, the population dropped by half to 15,334 by 1970. Among those who left were not only mining families but also other businessmen who could not stay solvent without the mining industry. Thus, this once-booming town is barely surviving as a city.

The Besshi Copper Mine in Uma-County, Ehime Prefecture, was one of the most prominent copper mines in Japan but will be closed in March, 1973. At the beginning of the Meiji Era, more than 10,000 people lived here, but the population gradually shrank as the ore reserves became smaller. Now, there are only about eight hundred people waiting for the mine to shut down. When the lights go out in the mines after nearly three centuries, what will happen to these villages which have shared their destiny with the mines?

The main reason for the declining population in most areas, however, is the shift of the farming population into secondary and tertiary industries. Needless to say, Japanese agriculture has come to an historic turning point. Since 1968, the supply of Japanese agriculture's principal product, rice, has been in excess of demand, and paddy acreage has had to be curbed. As the economy becomes more international, the demands from abroad for the liberalization of farm product imports will become stronger. In order to compete with foreign agriculture, we must make our agriculture more productive. From the viewpoint of domestic economic interests, too, farm income should be raised to the levels of the secondary and tertiary industries if we intend to secure future agricultural workers. Rural young have already left their homes *en masse*, and those elderly farmers who are left behind to till the land find it difficult to lead balanced social lives.

The 1971 White Paper on Agriculture puts the average annual per-household income in agriculture at $5,350. Of this total, only $1,690 is derived from farming, and the remaining $3,660, or nearly 60 percent, comes from non-agricultural activities. This demonstrates clearly that farmers can no longer live on agriculture alone.

This is why agricultural workers have to seek non-agricultural employment away from home. This practice is wide-spread, although it is naturally more characteristic of northern areas relying wholly upon their one rice harvest each year. Except in spring and fall, when the whole family is at work on the land, entire farm villages are made up of only old people and housewives. In Niigata Prefecture, there are even some all-women fire departments.

How can we expect to have the energy necessary to build tomorrow's Japan when rural villages include few young people, when couples must be separated for such long times, and when old people must do such strenuous work in villages without doctors?

2

Economic Growth for Social Welfare

Further Growth Is Necessary and Possible

The postwar Japanese economy has grown at an average annual rate of more than 10 percent in real terms. This rate of growth did not slacken even after the postwar recovery phase, as shown by the real growth rate of 11.1 percent in the 1960–1965 period. Such economic development is unique in man's history and has been looked upon as the "Japanese miracle." In seeking to explain this "miracle," experts have pointed out a number of factors:

1. The principle of peace has been consistently observed and arms expenditures have been kept to a minimum under the present Constitution.

2. Educational standards are high and an industrious labor force was abundant.

3. Technical innovation with the positive introduction of new technology and equipment resulted in higher productivity and enhanced Japan's international competitiveness.

4. The financial system supported vigorous corporate business operations, with Government playing a constructive role.

5. The liberal, multilateral, and non-discriminatory postwar world trade system proved favorable to Japan.

6. The Liberal Democratic Party has maintained political stability, keeping the support of a majority of the people.

As a result, a propitious "growth cycle" was formed in the economy. This cycle started with private plant and equipment investment, which in turn stimulated subsequent rounds of investment.

Still Great Potential

During the past several years, however, we have come to observe drastic changes in Japan's internal and external economic environments.

First, private plant and equipment investment, always the pillar of the "growth cycle," has shown signs of slackening. While the annual rate of growth of private investment was 14.8 percent between fiscal 1960 and fiscal 1970, this was down slightly in fiscal 1971 with a further drop estimated for fiscal 1972.

Secondly, exports are not likely to increase at the same rate as before. Exports have always been the leading factor in the postwar economic development, but foreign nations have become increasingly wary of expanded Japanese exports, and there have even developed moves aimed at restricting the flow of Japanese goods into their domestic markets.

Thirdly, overcrowding and environmental pollution in the big cities became serious in the high-growth period, and there is increasing citizen opposition to new industrial construction on the grounds that it will cause pollution. Some industries are even finding it increasingly difficult to locate new factories.

The fourth new factor is the shortage of labor, particularly young labor.

Citing these elements, many people now believe that the period of rapid growth for the Japanese economy is over. However, even though we may not be able to expect any large increase in either private plant and equipment investment or exports, there are still a number of factors sufficient to support continued economic growth.

The first is the expansion of infrastructure investment. The per-capita stock of social overhead capital as of 1970 amounted to $1,500. This is only one-third that of the U.S., five-eighths of Great Britain's, and two-thirds of West Germany's. Nationwide improvement of the infrastructure should be given top priority to prevent further population imbalances and environmental deterioration, to realize a higher standard of living and expanded industrial activity, and ultimately to build a beautiful Japan. To close the gap with the U.S. in this respect, it is estimated that social overhead capital investments on the order of $900 billion will have to be made during the 1970's. The people are also anxious to start with the more urgent projects, such as parks, playgrounds, sewage systems, garbage disposal facilities, medical facilities, roads, ports, and harbors.

The second factor supporting optimism for continued growth is the increase in personal consumption. The present per-capita personal consumption averages $738, which is only one-fourth of the U.S.'s and half of West Germany's or France's. But as national income rises and the standard of living improves, the people's wants will become more sophisticated and diversified.

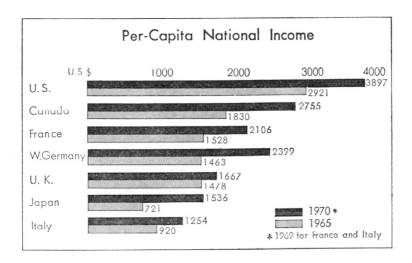

Per-Capita National Income

	1970*	1965
U.S.	3897	2921
Canada	2755	1830
France	2106	1528
W.Germany	2399	1463
U. K.	1667	1478
Japan	1536	721
Italy	1254	920

* 1969 for France and Italy

This should bring a drastic increase in personal consumption in such areas as housing and cultural or sporting activities. As to slackening private plant and equipment investment, we can expect increased expenditures for labor-saving, pollution prevention, safety, and other such purposes.

The third factor supporting continued growth is that Japan, with its highly capable population of more than one hundred million, under a free and democratic socio-economic system, can effectively direct its economy in a manner conducive to peace and international cooperation.

If we work to shift the traditional course of economic growth from one based on private investment and exports to one with the priority on welfare and increased social overhead expenditures, the economy still has great growth potential.

Welfare Is Not Heaven-Sent

There are some who claim that high growth is unnecessary,

that no more industrial development is needed, and that we should now improve social welfare. But it is wrong to postulate a choice between growth or welfare, industry or a better life. Social welfare will neither be heaven-sent nor be given as a gift from outside. Only the accumulations which come from economic growth through our own vitality can provide an adequate source of money.

If we should lower the rate of economic growth considerably, what would happen to our economy and society in general? First of all, construction of public facilities and housing would be relatively retarded, and personal income growth would be slowed. According to one estimate, annual pay raises of any substance would become almost impossible even after siphoning off a goodly portion of corporate reserves and profits to pay employees. With respect to foreign trade, a slackening economy would mean a large drop in raw materials imports which would betray the expectations of developing nations counting on these exports to Japan. If some industries should be forced to resort to vigorous export campaigns to offset unfavorable domestic sales, they would very likely create frictions in the international marketplace. Social security programs would also feel the pinch because there would be no increased revenue to finance them. If we are to conquer overcrowding and environmental pollution to build a pleasant and prosperous society, it is necessary to relocate industries, redevelop our overcrowded cities, improve social investment in road and sewage systems, and develop antipollution technologies. The vast amounts of funds needed for these projects cannot be secured in a low-growth economy. Unless, therefore, a system of reasonably rapid economic growth is assumed, it will be impossible to solve the numerous problems now facing the Japanese economy.

There is one argument which claims that a lower growth rate would halt rising prices. But the example of Great Britain proves the contrary. Britain's low rate of economic growth, 2.7 percent in real terms, has been accompanied by consumer price increases of 4.1 percent annually. President Nixon adopted a tight-money policy to hold down prices, but only ended up increasing unemployment without reducing prices. Since the summer of 1971, the U.S. has turned to promoting growth again.

It is true that there is such a thing as demand-pull inflation caused by a high growth rate and consequent strong demand. But that is not the main reason for our rising prices in Japan. Rather, Japan is troubled by so-called "productivity-gap inflation" caused by the fact that wages rise at the same rate for all industries regardless of their different productivities. To understand this, one need only note that price increases are concentrated in sectors where productivity has not improved as fast, such as farm products, small-business products, and services of various kinds.

It follows that the first step to stave off further price increases should be to increase the productivity of such low-productivity industries as agriculture, small- and medium-sized businesses, and services by promoting their modernization and rationalization. Secondly, distribution costs should be lowered through road and railway improvements and through sharp modernization of the distribution system. Still another measure to be taken is to lower the burden imposed by land prices by relocating industry and population to rural areas. Comprehensive execution of all of these measures is the only way to check further price increases.

Growth: A Double-Edged Sword

If the Japanese economy grows at an annual rate of 10 percent, using 1970's GNP of $243 billion as the base, GNP in 1985 will be one trillion dollars. While this seems to be a gargantuan figure, the wisdom of the Japanese people and the energy of their economy are the underlying powers to make this come true.

There are various views on the future growth rate of the economy. A 5-percent annual growth rate will bring the 1985 GNP to $507 billion (in 1970 prices). At 7.5 percent per annum, the corresponding figure will be $720 billion; and at 8.5 percent it will be $830 billion. The New Comprehensive National Development Plan gives an estimate of $430 to $500 billion for the 1985 GNP in 1965 prices. Converted into 1970 prices, it comes to around $670 billion, which corresponds roughly to 7.5 percent growth.

Given a GNP of one trillion dollars, the total production of all manufacturing industries will amount to $910 billion in real terms, and the industrial scale will be four times today's. Such production will require industrial sites totaling 1,100 square miles (as opposed to 480 square miles as of the end of 1969), as well as 93,700,000 tons of industrial water per day (against 44,700,000 tons in 1969). Goods to be transported will also increase four-fold from 1969's 220 billion ton-miles to 820 billion ton-miles.

National income will also increase greatly, and one estimate gives a figure of more than $10,000 (in terms of 1970 prices) as the average annual income per employee.

The question is how the four main islands of Japan, with a

GNP (Nominal) and Industrial Shipments

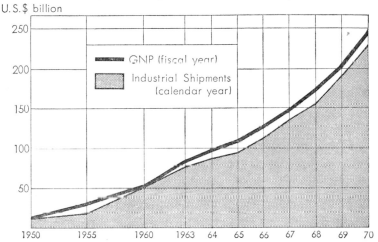

U.S.$ billion

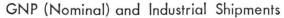

total land area of only one-twenty-fifth of the U.S.A., can afford an economy as large as today's U.S. economy. Such growth for the Japanese economy is a double-edged sword, capable of bringing good or evil. It is this choice of how to use our acquired riches that is thrust upon us.

From Energy-Consuming to Knowledge-Intensive Industries

During the decade of 1955–1965, economic policy for the industrial structure was overwhelmingly growth-oriented, with the priority on promoting heavy and chemical industries. These industries, with a high rate of increase in demand proportionate to increased income (or a greater income elasticity of demand) and rapidly rising productivity, have played an historic role as core industries leading the economy throughout the high-growth period. At the same time, however, it is equally true

65

that they have served to aggravate overcrowding and environmental pollution, as well as international friction in foreign trade.

The future industrial structure, then, should be chosen not only for growth but also from the viewpoint of making Japan a more pleasant and worthwhile country to live in. In other words, instead of just depending on the conventional heavy and chemical industries, the industries to lead the economy in the future should be selected using the criteria of how little damage they do to the environment (pollution-burden standards) and how much pride and pleasure they give their workers (labor environment standards).

Thus we can only conclude that the center of gravity of the new industrial structure should be changed from material- and energy-consuming heavy and chemical industries to knowledge-intensive industries making greater use of man's wisdom and knowledge. Since these industries consume relatively little in the way of raw materials and energy for their final products, they are less likely to cause pollution or otherwise destroy the environment. They can also provide the highly educated labor force with intellectually satisfying jobs instead of simple repetitive tasks, thereby making it possible for people to take pride and pleasure in their work. It is these knowledge-intensive industries which serve the cause of harmonious coexistence between industry and environment and are the key to recovering our humanity.

How can we achieve an industrial structure based on knowledge-intensive industries? We should develop R&D-intensive industries that utilize knowledge, technology, and ideas (computers, aircraft, electric automobiles, industrial robots, and marine development), sophisticated assembly industries (communications equipment, business machines, anti-pollution devices, and educational equipment), fashion industries (sophisticated clothing, furniture, and household utensils), and knowledge industries producing and marketing knowledge and information (information-processing services, video industrics, and systems engineering), and at the same time have other general manufacturing industries become more knowledge-intensive through process sophistication and product improvement. Advancing such a course of development requires that we develop new techniques and train personnel suited to the needs of the new age. In the knowledge-intensive industries, the quality and capability of people is the key factor in development. Of course, industries providing materials and energy in support of these new industries cannot be neglected, and they should be properly distributed throughout the Japanese archipelago. However, it is the knowledge-intensive industries that will assume the leadership in economic growth.

Ending the Distortions of Growth

The Japanese economy has so far been operated in a cyclical pattern of "growth pursuit," directing the strength gained through rapid development into private plant and equipment investment which in turn furthers growth. Government policy emphasized the maintenance and expansion of economic growth, and industry was primarily concerned with enlarging operational scale. As a result, the Government prided itself on increased GNP while private firms boasted of increased market share. In this climate, the Japanese economy grew to be one of the strongest in the world, and Japanese companies successfully enlarged their scale and strengthened their management. We have achieved increased per-capita income and a higher standard of living. The postwar economic history has undoubtedly been one of a successful economy.

But the domestic and international environments have undergone a fundamental change. We are now being asked not only to grow but also to make positive use of our greater economic strength for national welfare and international cooperation. This is a time when we must replace the pursuit of growth with the utilization of growth.

The period of rapid growth has given rise to such distortions as pollution, inflation, urban overcrowding, rural depopulation, and agricultural stagnation. To solve these problems and to provide a worthwhile life in a pleasant country, we must waste no time in improving social overhead capital and the social security standards.

Let us take education for example. We have a great number of colleges and universities, but facilities are inadequate for the great majority of students, and the educational environment is unsatisfactory. A nation's progress depends, after all, upon the quality of education. We must spare no effort in investing more money for educational purposes. It is our responsibility to see to it that students can enjoy a liberal education in a pleasant environment in order that they can be properly prepared for their future roles. National health is also very important. No village should be without a doctor, and hospital facilities should be improved with particular attention to the problems of the aged. Government provisions for social security should be improved in order to protect the physically handicapped, the aged, and the sick who cannot adapt to our rapidly changing society.

Only through positively utilizing our acquired economic strength in such ways can we achieve a better national life and social welfare. Only in this way can we break through to a new and propitious growth cycle.

Welfare Promotes Growth, and Growth Promotes Welfare

To get the Japanese economy back on the right track and to promote an economic policy of growth utilization, it is necessary to drastically alter Government fiscal policy. So far, we have stressed the importance of a balanced budget for each fiscal year. Although this is sound fiscal practice, it creates numerous problems in a rapidly growing economy such as ours. The revenue which is able to produce the size and capacity of today's Japanese economy is inadequate to carry out the projects called for by the expanding economy and society of Japan.

Let us consider a specific example. Suppose that a certain project takes seven years from the planning stage to completion. If the economy grows at an average annual rate of 10 percent, it will double its size in the seven years. If, therefore, the project is surveyed and started in accordance with the revenue in its initial fiscal year, it will already be too small when it is completed. Public facilities should generally be planned some fifteen years ahead, but so long as the idea of balanced financing prevails, it will be impossible to make the necessary social overhead capital improvements.

Until recently, fiscal expansion had been likely to overheat the economy or to bring about serious balance-of-payments deficits. But these fears have been eliminated as Japan's productive capacity has grown and large foreign-currency reserves have been accumulated. We should, therefore, free ourselves from the idea of annually balanced budgets and place more importance on balanced public finance over the long run. We must set forth a positive fiscal policy taking into consideration not only the burden on the present generation but also the burden on future generations. While it seems a kindly gesture to leave no debts behind, debts are not in themselves inherently evil. If the land is passed to succeeding generations without the necessary infrastructure investments having been made, it will obviously create impediments to their life and industrial activities. A fair distribution of the costs among generations is necessary if we are to build a beautiful and pleasant nation to live in.

Such positive public financing will not only lead to a richer social overhead, better education and medical care, and faster technological development; it will also stimulate the economy to further growth. This is because it will contribute directly to increased demand through expanded public investment and income redistribution, and will also have many economic side-effects. Railway and road improvement will increase the land availability, which in turn will provide opportunities for housing construction. Expanded social security with fewer worries about old age will increase spending for consumer goods. When new techniques for pollution control, housing, transportation, education, and medicine are more widely applied, new knowledge-intensive industries will be forthcoming.

Thus, the use of a growth-utilization pattern in the management of economy will create a propitious cycle where welfare promotes growth and growth promises greater welfare.

Japan's Role in the World Community

Lacking significant natural resources and with a population of over one hundred million people, Japan has always followed a trade pattern of importing energy resources and industrial materials and exporting finished goods with new value added. It is thanks to its efforts as a trading nation that Japan has come to occupy a conspicuous position within the fast-growth sector of the free world, along with the U.S. and Europe. In the process, Japan's share of free-world trade has rapidly increased. The ratio of Japanese exports to total free-world exports was 6.9 percent in 1970, nearly double the figure of one decade before, ranking Japan third after the U.S. and West Germany. The rapid development of our trade is, of course, due to the great efforts of the Japanese people, but at the same time it is also due to the existence of a free, multilateral, and non-discriminatory international economic system which has worked in favor of postwar Japan.

Recently, however, criticism has been voiced by other nations of the world that Japan's rapid economic development constitutes a violation of the "speed limits" of the international economic race. Movements to restrict imports of Japanese goods have surfaced in certain quarters in the United States and Europe. I am concerned that international trade may turn from efforts to balance trade disequilibriums by expanding exports to efforts to limit imports.

Until recently, we have remained a quiet participant in the existing international economic order of the Bretton Woods system and GATT and concentrated on adapting our own economic system to that order. But today's Japan is a prominent economic power whose slightest actions may have major international repercussions. We can no longer take a passive stand and evade our expected roles and responsibilities which we feel we should now assume. The international economic order is in the midst of a painful readjustment, as can be seen by the

North-South problem and the international monetary problem. In cooperation with the United States and Europe, we must act in a positive manner to establish a new world order for peace and international cooperation.

Even though there may be some conflicts of interest between Japan and the rest of the world, we will be able to solve our problems through negotiations so long as we have the common objective of contributing to international economic development and peace. The important thing is to maintain at all times a general climate receptive to frank discussions. Japan cannot live without peace, and the gigantic Japanese economy can continue to grow only in a peaceful international environment. In this context, it is important for us to strive for a world order under which our rapid economic growth may contribute directly to international economic development, extending our prosperity to the rest of the world,

During the 1960's, the developing nations of the "South" achieved an average growth rate of 5.5 percent, a record superior to the corresponding figure of 4.8 percent for the advanced countries. But because of the explosive population increases in the "South," the difference in per-capita income became still wider. Additionally, a new "North-South problem" within the "South" has arisen between those developing nations that have achieved industrialization and others that have been left behind. In the United Nations' Second Development Decade starting in 1971, international cooperation was taken up as a common task for the entire world, and the third U.N. Conference on Trade and Development (UNCTAD) held in Santiago talked of raising official development assistance from the advanced nations to 0.7 percent of their GNP.

While the East-West problem is being reduced by peaceful

coexistence, the North-South problem has become the most important task for the remaining thirty years of this century. Japan's new development will depend upon how well we can contribute to the economic independence and better life of the developing countries.

Japan extended $1,820,000,000 in economic aid to the developing nations in 1970 (0.93 percent of GNP), and $460,000,000 (0.23 percent of GNP) of this was official aid. By 1980, our economic aid must be increased to over $7.5 billion. Recipient nations should naturally include all countries of Asia, Africa, and Latin America with which Japan has relations. Particularly toward Asian countries, we must honestly reexamine past practices, which have tended to be oriented toward our own gain, and work sincerely for a flexible assistance pattern truly in keeping with the conditions and interests of individual recipient countries. The time is past when a few advanced economic powers can discuss and decide international economic problems. In order to seek the path of equality, reciprocity, and prosperity, listening to the demands of the developing nations for a fair and rational readjustment of the international division of labor, we should improve Japan's industrial structure, make the necessary domestic reforms to promote better regional balance, and direct our growing economic strength to the assistance of all "Southern" nations.

PART II

Rechanneling the Flow of People and Economy

3

Relocating Industries

Moving Against Overcrowding and Underpopulation Together

It is possible to transform Japan into a richer, less polluted, and more livable land than it is now. To do this, however, it is necessary to divert the historical trend concentrating industry, population, and culture in the major urban areas and to refocus the development emphasis on outlying regions.

In so doing, long-term and comprehensive planning to improve pump-priming social overhead capital is most important. At the same time, it would also be effective to locate new industries and relocate existing industries to local areas in line with those areas' developmental potential. Industry is both the detonator and the guiding force for regional development.

Many precedents exist, but only for very simple introduction of industry into rural areas, such as the New Industrial Cities,

Special Areas for Industrial Consolidation, Coal Mining Developing Areas, and Rural Industrialization Plans.

What I mean here by industrial relocation is to halt the flow of industry into the Pacific coastal region and to actively divert industry from the overcrowded urban areas to rural sites. In other words, this means taking from Tokyo, Osaka, and other urban concentrations their traditional industrial function and dispersing these industries from a national perspective. The pump primed with the scattering of secondary industry to rural areas, this will also lead to a nation-wide redistribution of tertiary industries and the improvement of productivity in the primary sector.

Thus the redistribution of industry is an integral and pivotal part of the comprehensive national development plan including building a nation-wide network of super-express railways, providing expressways and other highway transport facilities, constructing connecting bridges between Shikoku and Honshu, forming a nation-wide information and communications network, protecting the environment, redeveloping our urban areas, creating regional urban centers, and restoring Japanese agriculture.

The many distortions now being generated in Japan are indeed serious, as noted in Chapter 1. Yet if urbanization continues unchecked, land, housing, labor, and water problems will become still more difficult in urban areas, and pollution and traffic problems will get still worse. Even if water and labor are somehow made available, their costs will be economically prohibitive. Yet to improve only the urban areas would be to create a new and uncontrollable influx of population in search of this heightened urban convenience. Moreover, workers coming to these urban areas will, except for the young unmarrieds, bring

Overall Policy for National Land Development

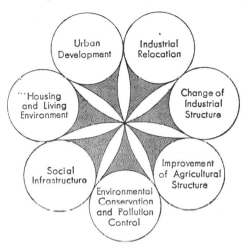

their families with them. When these people begin to look for homes and begin life within the urban society, the government's expenditures on them will also increase. Yet the effect of excessive expenditures in such non-productive sectors would be to sap the energies necessary for economic growth, resulting in a poorer functioning of the Japanese economy and a lower standard of living. If the problems are to be solved, urban reconstruction and rural development must be pursued simultaneously. Overpopulation and underpopulation must be solved concurrently and the country must be rebuilt into a highly efficient and balanced one. Industrial relocation can provide powerful leverage to this end.

Even assuming that the Japanese GNP reaches one trillion dollars by 1985, the nation possesses sufficient physical space to accommodate such an enormous economy. With a total land area of 142,000 square miles, the Japanese islands are currently divided into roughly 23,000 square miles of agricultural land, 2,500 square miles of residential land, 500 square miles of industrial-use land, 101,000 square miles of wilderness, and open space. Assuming that industrial shipments will reach $910 billion by 1985, approximately 1,120 square miles will be required for industrial uses. Thus slightly over 1,200 square miles will suffice even allowing for green belts, recreational playgrounds, and parks around these industrial sites. This is a mere one percent of the total land available.

There is a plan within the government to set aside 20 to 30 percent of the nation's area as environmental conservation areas. Setting aside the question of which specific areas are selected as environmental conservation areas, it is entirely possible to fulfill the goals of industrial development while still preserving Japan's natural beauty, conserving wilderness and farmlands, and meeting the growing demand for housing.

At present, some 32 percent of the total Japanese population is living on that less than one percent of the land area enclosed within 30-mile radii of Tokyo, Osaka, and Nagoya. While it is true that Japan is short of good residential land, it is certainly feasible to expand the living area through regional development. Looking at the problem of water resources, too, it will be entirely possible to meet the water demands of the one trillion dollar economy by raising the river utilization rate from its present 16 percent to 21 percent.

Looking at the labor force, people engaged in primary industries account for a high 17.4 percent of the total working population of Japan. If it is possible to reduce this to about 7 percent by 1985, with industrial redistribution and a comprehensive agricultural policy, this will release some eight million workers for participation in secondary and tertiary industries.

In March of 1971, the Ministry of International Trade and Industry and the Ministry of Agriculture and Forestry joined together to sponsor the Law for the Promotion of Industrialization of Farm Areas. This was followed by the enactment of the Industrial Relocation Promotion Law which carried these principles one step further. The cumulative result was a perfect meshing of industrial relocation and agricultural policies. With the implementation of these policies, it will be possible for surplus labor leaving agriculture to stay in the local area and shift easily to secondary or tertiary employment. Since these workers will live with their families, they will be able to grow a little rice or vegetables for themselves and to commute to work from their own homes. Until this is done, there can be no end to the tragedy of men having to leave home to find employment, leaving their wives at home to lament, "I'd rather have him here, even if he only made half as much."

By 1985, the Japanese population will reach approximately 120 million and it is estimated that more than 80 percent of these people will be leading urban lives if things continue their present course. Yet "leading urban lives" need not necessarily mean that they will be in Tokyo, Osaka, or the other existing megalopolises. If regional development is initiated and promoted through industrial relocation so as to generate jobs in nonmetropolitan areas, raise local income levels, create parks, sewage systems, and other amenities of the living environment, and provide a superior social environment including adequate medical, cultural, and recreational facilities, surely it may be expected that people will want to settle there. Only this will open the door to orderly urban development and mutual prosperity for both farm and city. It is precisely such far-sighted investment which will bring the highest returns in the long run.

New Concept for Industrial Parks

Industrial relocation, a policy based on a macroscopic perspective, stems from a desire to eliminate the existing disparity between the Pacific coastal belt and the other regions of Japan. Calling for the construction of a nation-wide network of super-express railways and expressways to create a vast exodus of industry from the Pacific metropolitan areas to remote areas, including the Japan Sea coast, and to bring new industry to these regions, these policies are aimed at reducing the Pacific coast's share of all industrial shipments from its present 73 percent to 50 percent by 1985. To be more specific, it is intended to designate the built-up districts of the National Capital Sphere and metropolitan urban area of the Kinki region (although the handling of the Chubu region has yet to be decided) as Industrial Departure Promotion Areas to shift industry out of these overindustrialized regions, and to halve the area of industrial sites in these areas to approximately 40 square miles.

In addition, the Tohoku, Hokuriku, San'in, Shikoku, and Kyushu regions, as well as Hokkaido, Okinawa, and other select prefectures, are to be designated Industrial Relocation Reception Areas for those industries leaving the overindustrialized Pacific coast and for new industries wishing to locate there.

In advancing this industrial relocation, however, there must be a full exchange of views between the central government, the local governments, and residents on the details of planning and implementation, and all work must await the understanding and consent of the area's residents. This principle cannot be overstressed.

As well as raising the value added, reducing pollution, saving labor, and conserving resources, the knowledge-intensive orientation of industrial policies in the 1970's is also aimed at reducing the burden on the land and the environment. Accordingly, the question of how to locate these highly knowledge-intensive inland industries is an extremely important one for future industrial location policies. At the same time, we must not neglect the basic resource-consuming industries which provide the foundation for the knowledge-intensive industries. There are basically two main parts in the new industrial map of Japan drawn by this industrial relocation.

Northeast and Southwest Passage

The first part is the location of those basic resource-consuming industries, which provide materials and energy for all industries. Iron and steel, non-ferrous metals, petroleum refining, petrochemicals, and electrical power are all representative of this field. Logically these can be located in Japan's northeast and southwest. These areas are blessed with favorable sites for the construction of large-scale industrial bases, such as Eastern Tomakomai (Hokkaido), Mutsu-Ogawara (Aomori Prefecture), and Akita Bay (Akita Prefecture) in the northeast and Suo-Nada Coast (Yamaguchi, Fukuoka, and Oita Prefectures) and Shibushi Bay (Kagoshima Prefecture) in the southwest.

Yet why locate massive bases for these basic, resource-consuming industries in the northeast and southwest of Japan far from Tokyo, Osaka, and Nagoya? Assuming the advent of the one trillion dollar economy, it is estimated that the demand for products of these industries will reach 200 million tons of crude steel, 15 million barrels of refined petroleum (198 billion gallons annually), and 17 million tons of petrochemical products (figured on an ethelyne-equivalency basis). This means vast expansions in industrial capacity to two times current crude steel levels, four times for refined petroleum, and four times for petrochemicals.

However, conservative estimates of ultimate steel production with new and expanded facilities on the industry's present sites place output at no more than 160 million tons of crude steel. Thus the remaining 40 million tons must be produced at new facilities in new locations if 1985's estimated 200 million ton demand is to be met. If we decide to turn to imports rather than expanding domestic steel production, of course, these new locations will not be needed, but Japanese steel is the lowest-priced in the world, and it would hardly be realistic to propose going out of our way to import more expensive foreign steels.

By the same token, the most that the oil refining industry can possibly process on its present sites is 8 million barrels of crude oil, and the petrochemical industry has an ultimate limit of 5,500,000 tons on an ethylene-equivalency basis. Unlike the steel situation, part of the demand for petroleum and petro-chemical products is currently being met with imports. While these imports can be increased, perhaps up to 2 million barrels of petroleum and 2 million tons of petrochemicals (ethylene equivalency), it will still be necessary to seek new sites to process 5 million barrels of petroleum and to produce 9,500,000 tons (ethylene equivalency) of petrochemical products by 1985. Moreover, it is highly problematical whether the planned expansion of facilities at current sites can be allowed in view of the worsening pollution and overcrowding.

These basic, resource-consuming industries are also capital-

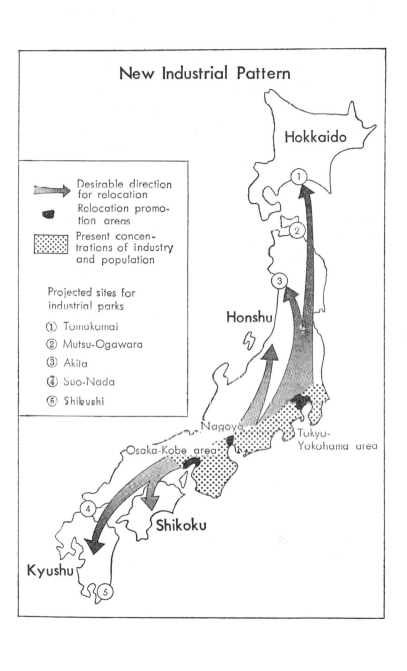

New Industrial Pattern

Desirable direction for relocation

Relocation promotion areas

Present concentrations of industry and population

Projected sites for industrial parks

① Tomakomai
② Mutsu-Ogawara
③ Akita
④ Suo-Nada
⑤ Shibushi

Hokkaido

Honshu

Nagoya

Osaka-Kobe area

Tokyo-Yokohama area

Shikoku

Kyushu

intensive and are constantly expanding to take advantage of economies of scale and the benefits of continuing technological innovation. Thus common sense demands that they be situated in complexes linking iron and steel, chemicals, and electrical power or joining petroleum, petrochemicals, and electrical power to integrate the entire production cycle from raw material to finished product. It is anticipated that the plants put into operation by 1985 will have production and processing capacities of 20 million tons annually for crude steel, one million barrels for crude oil, and 2 million tons for petrochemicals (ethylene-equivalency). Quick calculations using these figures show that the steel industry will need two new giant steel works, the petroleum industry five major refineries, and the petrochemical industry five new ethylene centers by 1985. And since these will form the nuclei of huge new complexes, land needs will be substantial indeed.

The most important thing here is to give priority consideration to the safety and welfare of local residents and industrial workers by providing comprehensive anti-pollution measures, protecting the environment, and working to prevent industrial disasters. These cannot be complexes simply for production's sake but must be well laid out with ample room for better living. The new mammoth industrial bases at Eastern Tomakomai and Mutsu-Ogawara will naturally be larger in scale than even the Kashima Coastal Industrial Region (some 13 square miles of industrial sites alone). In addition, major ports will be needed capable of accommodating massive tankers and ore carriers drawing 100 to 130 feet which will be necessary to carry the vast amounts of crude oil, iron ore, bauxite, etc., which must be purchased abroad.

Since these industries will also use vast amounts of water,

they must be located where the needed water, including sea water, can be secured. In this connection, it should be noted that 70 percent of Japan's industrial water is used by the iron and steel, chemicals, and paper and pulp industries. Providing just 5 million tons of crude steel (a medium-size works as steel works go) takes as much water as all of the 7,600,000 people living in Osaka Prefecture use in one year. It is obvious that the possible locations for these vast, basic resource-consuming industrial bases are inherently limited by natural conditions.

Neither Tokyo Bay nor Osaka Bay is able to accommodate 500,000-ton tankers. And even if they could, the already aggravated pollution and environmental disruptions caused by overpopulation make it impermissible that new industrial complexes should be located in or around these urban areas. The only places left for building new large-scale industrial complexes where it will be possible to secure the necessary industrial water and where land is still relatively inexpensive are in the northeast and southwest.

Already the plans for a new petroleum complex in Futtsu (Chiba Prefecture) on Tokyo Bay have encountered strong opposition from local residents and will likely be forced to relocate elsewhere. This means that sites for new complexes must be adequate not only to meet increasing requirements in future, but also to accommodate both expansion planned at urban sites, and the existing plants which are themselves being moved out of their overcrowded settings. In the long run, this means scrapping the existing industrial areas in Tokyo, Osaka, and elsewhere and building anew in remote areas. In this sense, the construction of new industrial bases holds great promise for the future.

Shifting our focus from the large-scale to the smaller industrial bases, it is clear that shipbuilding, heavy machinery, foodstuffs, timber-related, and other industrial complexes heavily dependent upon marine transport and using vast amounts of industrial water must also be located along the Japanese coast. Most of these are medium-sized, distribution-processing complexes requiring sites of four to six square miles. Likely candidates for these medium industrial complexes are Tachibana Bay (Tokushima Prefecture), Sukumo Bay (Kochi Prefecture), Ariake (Saga, Fukuoka, and Kumamoto Prefectures), Yatsu-shiro (Kumamoto Prefecture), Nakaumi (Tottori and Shimane Prefectures), Fukui New Port (Fukui Prefecture), Niigata East Port (Niigata Prefecture), Sakata New Port (Yamagata Prefecture), Hakodate Bay (Hokkaido), Ishikari New Port (Hokkaido), Kita-Kanto New Port (Ibaraki Prefecture), Nakananse (Mie Prefecture), Nakagusuku Bay (Okinawa Prefecture), Kin Bay (Okinawa Prefecture), etc.

Bringing the Factory to the Farm

The other major trend contributing to this new industrial map of Japan is the development of inland industries in agricultural regions. This includes the machinery industry, most electronics, and systems industries such as medical equipment, household appliances, and the like. Compared with the industries located along the coast, these labor-intensive industries use little water but have high productivity in terms of value added by manufacture. Roads and railways are their major means of transportation. Among the many products which these industries turn out are color television sets, tape-recorders, stereo sets, data communications equipment, computers, desk-top calculators, business machines, traffic signal and safety equipment, fire-alarm systems, pollution-prevention devices, automobiles, motorcycles, cultivators, planters, combines, driers, elevators, escalators, cranes, conveyers, machine tools, plastic-processing equipment, food-processing equipment, wood-working machinery, metal products for construction, room heaters and air conditioners, electrical lighting appliances, industrial meters, precision gauges, clocks and watches, cameras, lenses, toys, sporting goods, and a wide range of similar products.

During the process of developing heavy and chemical industries in Japan during the decade and a half from 1955 to 1970, almost all of these new productive facilities were located in coastal regions. All of the fifteen New Industrial Cities (Do'o, Hachinohe, Sendai Bay, Akita Bay, Joban-Koriyama, Niigata, Matsumoto-Suwa, Toyama-Takaoka, Nakaumi, Southern Okayama Prefecture, Tokushima, Toyo, Oita, Hyuga-Nobeoka, and Shiranui-Ariake-Omuta), with the exception of Matsumoto-Suwa, and all six of the Special Areas for Industrial Consolidation (Kashima, Higashi-Suruga Bay, Higashi-Mikawa, Harima, Bingo, and Shunan), are located in coastal or adjacent areas. The attitude toward inland location, however, has undergone considerable change over the past year or two. One reason for this has been the stagnation of plant and equipment investment in basic industries, which were heavily hit by the current recession. A far more important factor, though, has been the growing appreciation that the inland industries, being knowledge-intensive and in areas which will continue to grow rapidly as part of the increasingly sophisticated industrial structure, will have a major role to play in Japan's development.

Looking ahead to 1985, it has been estimated that, of Japan's total industrial shipments, the share of the basic, resource-consuming industries in the coastal areas will drop to 20 percent, while the inland industries' share will jump to 80 percent.

The Law to Promote Relocation of Industry in Agrarian Regions, enacted in 1971, sets forth plans to designate as rural areas 2,596 of Japan's 3,248 cities, towns, and villages, excluding those suburban to major cities, New Industrial Cities, large cities, etc., and to bring into these areas industries capable of making shipments totaling $30 billion by 1975. This would require some 60 square miles of factory sites and would employ approximately one million workers, of whom 600,000 are expected to be from farm families.

From the viewpoint of industry, land is expensive and labor scarce in the metropolitan areas. In the cities, where one square foot of land costs as much as $10 to $20, it is hard to make new plant expansion pay. Salaries in and around the big cities are 30 to 40 percent more than those elsewhere. Moreover, the competition to recruit the necessary employees has become intense. For each applicant, there are 1.6 to 2.7 jobs available now, thus making it difficult to recruit even half of the necessary labor force. On top of this, an increasing number of workers are seeking to leave this "industrial wasteland" in favor of pleasant residential surroundings and in search of work they feel has meaning. In the first place, land usage patterns in the major urban areas have not been systematically developed. The restrictions on converting agricultural land embodied in the Agricultural Land Law have been strict, and conversion has often been permitted for the convenience of agriculture alone, giving this system little relation to planned urban development. Industry too has moved almost exclusively to lower-priced land, giving rise to the sprawl phenomenon around Japan's big cities. As the cities have grown larger, factories once situated among fields become increasingly surrounded by private homes. And then begin the complaints about the noise, vibration, or noxious odors from the factory, which soon is forced to cease night-shift operations. Public opinion will not accept a simple "We were here first" stress on vested rights by the factory.

From the farmers' viewpoint, they too must find employment for their surplus labor which is generated by the decline in acreage farmed and must maintain their income level. At the same time, it has become necessary to make Japanese agriculture highly efficient and highly productive, capable of successfully coping with international competition. For this too, integration of agriculture and industry by introducing inland industries into agricultural areas is of particular importance.

For the large-scale coastal industrial bases, the most important condition for location is to secure wide expanses of land, abundant water, and spacious port facilities. The inland industries, on the other hand, can easily be dispersed throughout the country in search of their three major conditions of location: adequate transportation, such as highways and railways; urban services, such as housing, shopping areas, playgrounds, schools, and hospitals; and labor availability. An important key to the success or failure of regional development is the question of how well prepared these areas are to receive new industries, in terms of building regional centers, constructing automobile expressways and a national network of super-express railways, and improving ports and harbors. It is only natural that these inland industries, producing numerous processed and assembled products, should rely heavily upon trailer trucks and container vans for their transportation. Accordingly, the role of highways is crucial to locating inland industries.

There will be two principal approaches to rural industrialization. One will be the creation of focal points for broader regional development. This approach will be to build industrial parks in regions which have already accumulated some urban services and to locate factories in clusters. The other approach will be to move individual factories into rural villages on a one-village-one-factory basis. While the one-village-one-factory formula may be practical as a transitional step, the long-range perspective demands primary emphasis on the focal-point development approach. Typically, the local cities already central to regional economic activities, near expressway interchanges, could be improved to attract inland industrial parks. The appropriate size for such local cities would be a population of about 250,000.

If one superimposes the current expressway construction plans on a map showing existing local cities with adequate urban service, it is easy to see how inland industrial cities could be developed at such locations as Tsuyama (Okayama Prefecture), Niimi (Okayama Prefecture), Yokote (Akita Prefecture), Sakata-Tsuruoka (Yamagata Prefecture), Sanjo-Nagaoka (Niigata Prefecture), Takefu (Fukui Prefecture), Fukuchiyama (Kyoto Prefecture), and Miyakonojo (Miyazaki Prefecture). In implementing this concept, it goes without saying that the choice of industry should conform with local traditions and social or geographic conditions, and efforts must be made to preserve harmony with the indigenous industry.

What will the total flow of Japanese industry be like when the basic resource-consuming industries are redistributed along the northeast and southwest coasts and the high-value-added industries are located in inland rural areas? Until now the National Capital Sphere, Kinki region, and Chubu region have processed raw materials, produced goods, consumed them, and distributed them to the rest of the country. But after the industrial redistribution is completed, the pattern will be one of processing raw materials in the vast coastal industrial bases, manufacturing inland, and consuming nation-wide. At the same time, the national network of super-express railways and vehicle expressways will not work to siphon people from the countryside into the cities, but rather to carry people, centrifugally, from the urban centers to the countryside.

Industrializing for Cold and Snowy Areas

There is, however, deep-rooted opposition to this concept of industry relocation because of climatic conditions. Some people claim that the Japan Sea coast, Tohoku, or Hokkaido are not appropriate for industrialization because the weather is very cold and there are heavy snows. The fallacy of this claim can be seen simply by looking at the first page of any world atlas. Of the world's one hundred and forty nations, eleven of the advanced industrial nations, including the Soviet Union, are farther north than Japan. The industrial belt of the world is between 40 and 50 degrees latitude north. In Japan, Hachirogata in Akita Prefecture is the point 40 degrees north, and the 50-degree-north line runs through central Sakhalin far north of Japan's northernmost point.

In Europe, the powerful heavy industrial region of Saar-Ruhr is about 50 degrees north latitude, and England's Manchester and Liverpool are located about 52 degrees north and 53 degrees north latitudes, respectively. The world's industrial nations use their southern regions for agriculture and their northern regions for industrialization. The south has long hours of sunshine and is warm and fertile and well-suited for agriculture. The north has short daylight hours and snow and ice in winter, but this does not interfere with industry. Heavy and chemical industries in the United States are clustered

Major Industrial Concentrations

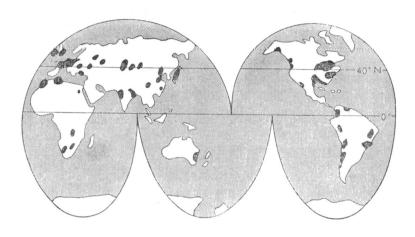

around or near the Great Lakes. Such major industrial cities as Chicago, Detroit, Pittsburgh, and Rochester are all near one or more of these lakes. By contrast, the southern United States is traditionally agricultural. In fact, a quick look at U.S. history shows that this conflict of interests between the newly industrialized north and the traditionally agricultural south was among the causes of the Civil War.

Now in the case of Japan, we have been using the warmer regions for industry and the colder areas for agriculture. There is no need to stick to this pattern. In some ways, it is that half of Japan which has heavy snowfall and is capable of producing only one crop a year which is best suited to industrialization. Water is abundantly available from the natural storehouse of the snows, land is plentiful, and there is an excellent potential labor force. Moreover, the geographical location of industrial sites on the Japan Sea or in Hokkaido will become even more advantageous when Japanese-Soviet cooperation in developing Siberia gets going, through projects such as Tyumen's oilfields, Sakhalin's natural gas and petroleum, and Udokan's copper ore. When the plan to build a steel works on the Shimokita Peninsula in Aomori Prefecture unfortunately failed to materialized, I told the parties concerned not to let go of the land, because they would just have to buy it back later at a higher price. Events since then have proven my forecast correct. And I would like to take this opportunity to predict once again that the Japan Sea coast and Hokkaido will have their day. Making a quick check of the development possibilities for the different areas based on the above reasoning, a blueprint for industrial redistribution begins to take shape.

Industrial shipments from the Kanto area now account for 36.4 percent of the national total. If industrial location trends are extrapolated in a straight line, this will be 43.9 percent, or nearly half, of the nation's industrial shipments by 1985. But, if industrial relocation targets are achieved, this will fall to 24.9 percent. By the same token, the share for the Kinki region will fall from 22.8 percent to 14.5 percent, instead of going up to 23.9 percent.

The Tohoku region now accounts for a mere 4.6 percent of the national total. Left to itself, this will drop to 3.2 percent, but with industrial relocation it can be raised to 13.3 percent. It will also be possible to boost Hokkaido's 2.2 percent to 5.8 percent and Kyushu's 5.0 percent to 11.4 percent. Since the absolute value of industrial shipments will increase four-fold during this period, Hokkaido and Hokuriku will show more than a ten-fold increase in absolute terms.

Industry Without Pollution

It will be impossible for future regional development to proceed unless it is done without disrupting the living environment of residents and with careful attention to conserving nature. How to solve industrial pollution problems has today become an important concern, going beyond just the construction of industrial complexes to include the survival of industry itself. Until several years ago, land prices were the main obstacle to the development of regional industries. Recently, however, an increasing number of people have come to feel that development means pollution and that more industrial development is unnecessary. While I can sympathize with such feelings, this chain of thought tends to overemphasize the disadvantages of development and overlook its many advantages. At times, it may even jump to the conclusion that a choice must be made between development or conservation, between industry or life.

The fact is, our life is not so simple as to permit an either-or choice. Electric power is one good example. Already, there is virtually no surplus electrical capacity. In this situation, what would become of our life if we were to stop all power development projects simply because they pollute the air? It is expected that home demand for electricity for lighting, television, refrigerators, air conditioners, room heaters, and so forth will expand faster than industrial demand. Great amounts of electrical energy are also used in transportation and communications and for other public services indispensable to the national livelihood, such as schools, nurseries, hospitals, subways, super-express trains, etc. If it becomes a question of whether we are supposed to put up with power failures simply to preserve nature untouched, I would say that this is not a realistic answer. For ages, we have been familiar with people who pass their unwanted problems on to their neighbors. This way of thinking is reflected today by the refusal of residents to permit the building of a garbage incineration plant, because of its smoke and odor, but who have no qualms at all about having it built in a neighboring town. This is no way to solve the problem. It is essential that we carry on development, and protect the citizens' living environment and conserve nature at the same time. I believe it is possible both to control pollution and to initiate development if we make effective use of the Japanese people's wisdom and scientific and technological progress. The regional dispersion of industry does not mean, and must not be allowed to mean, the regional dispersion of pollution.

Generally speaking, the source of pollutants in the air and water from which life itself springs is largely the basic resource-consuming industries by any standard. In order to eliminate pollution and create clean industrial complexes so that the nearby residents no longer have to worry, it is first necessary to do thorough research on pollution prevention and environmental harmony and to incorporate these systems into the formulation of basic plans for the construction of industrial bases.

The Yokkaichi complex marked an epoch in the postwar construction of heavy and chemical industrial bases. Industry spontaneously developed on the site where the old Imperial Navy Fuel Depot had been. While the choice of the site by the industries moving in may have been a well planned one from the viewpoint of production, it was grossly inadequate in providing harmony with the environment. The result was the serious pollution of the air, a deterioration in the health of the people, and a major social problem in the form of "Yokkaichi asthma."

97

There is an old saying that when you see a cart tip over on the road ahead, take a lesson from it. We must not repeat the tragedy of having our people fall victim to pollution. If plans to prevent pollution are formulated well ahead of the construction of industrial bases, it will be possible to reduce pollution to levels far below current levels when the complexes begin operation. This will eliminate pollution-related ailments. In order to do this, it is necessary to formulate an overall system of pollution controls, estimating nature's cleansing capacity and the volume of pollutants generated by industry and then calculating the maximum pollution-abating capability of existing and future techniques as well as cost factors involved.

As long as there is only a little organic matter in the water, animal plankton which feed on this are able to convert it into inorganic matter. This inorganic matter is then absorbed by vegetable plankton and in turn contributes to the photosynthetic production of oxygen. This is one example of nature's cleansing effect. But this natural purification capacity is not infinite. It does not follow that nature can necessarily remove pollutants and recycle our resources back to us just because we build taller smokestacks or dilute our industrial effluents. While building a higher smokestack does spread the smoke over a wider area and has a certain dispersion effect, the amount of sulfurous acid gas and nitrogen oxides in the air will continue to accumulate if the emitted pollution exceeds nature's capacity to cleanse. Using vast amounts of water to lower the concentration of industrial effluents will have a diluting effect. But the portion which exceeds nature's cleansing capacity will accumulate over the long run. As the accumulation of organic matter in the water increases, the oxygen level declines and it becomes impossible for fish to survive. There is also the very real danger of pollution through the food chain. Shellfish and small fish eat contaminated plankton in the water; these in turn are eaten by larger fish, which are eaten by man. As this cycle is repeated, the toxic substances accumulate in man's body and cause the various pollution-related ailments.

Pollution Controls

Therefore, the first requirement in constructing a large-scale industrial base is to hold total pollutant emission to within nature's cleansing capacity. Controls on the concentrations of pollutants which place no restrictions on the total amount of pollution so long as it is diluted are insufficient. Unless we take these regulations one step further and enact comprehensive restrictions holding down the absolute volume of pollutants generated, we will never be able to solve the problem of environmental disruption. Before constructing a major industrial base, we must formulate overall pollution control standards scientifically for each prospective site, ensuring that every industrial base is able to meet the standards.

The conventional approach of the Ministry of International Trade and Industry (MITI) has been to conduct Overall Pollution Prevention Surveys, which are designed to identify factors which should be monitored in pollution prevention, and then to formulate countermeasures. This has included investigating wind speeds, wind directions, and climatic changes for the industrial areas season by season, estimating the atmospheric dispersal capacity, and then calculating the smokestack height or fuel composition necessary to prevent pollution. If it is a coastal area, tides, water levels, wave patterns, water depths, and so forth are studied in order to predict how the effluent will be diluted in the sea, and to determine discharge sites and effluent concentrations based on this.

In the future, we will have to develop a comprehensive system incorporating both pollution-prevention techniques and economic cost factors in order to harmonize industrial bases with the broader environment. For example, if the sulfur content in crude oil is removed using the direct desulfurization method, it is possible with present technology to reduce the sulfur content in heavy and crude oil to about 0.7 percent. The oil which Japan presently imports has a high sulfur content of between 2 and 3 percent. The cost of reducing this to 0.7 percent through direct desulfurization is said to be about $3.30 to $8 per ton. If the gaseous desulfurization method is used, it is possible to reduce the sulfur content in heavy and crude oil to 0.05 percent, but the costs incurred run from $6.60 to $10 per ton. Thus, during the planning stage for a new industrial base, we should decide whether or not to increase petroleum refining capacity to one million barrels or to hold it to about 500,000 barrels on the basis of a comprehensive evaluation of the amount of sulfurous acid gas generated, the atmospheric dispersal range, nature's natural cleansing capacity, desulfurization costs, etc. Even granting that nature's capacity to cleanse will not change, desulfurization techniques can be improved and costs reduced so that, once the land for the industrial base is secured, it will be possible to operate at the 500,000 barrel level initially and later expand this to one million barrels.

Technological Innovation and Green Belts

Positive action to install anti-pollution devices must be taken by industries participating in developing industrial bases if they are to meet the overall emission control standards established. The adoption of such measures as desulfurization, direct and indirect, which depend on the nature of the fuel, should be made obligatory in order to eliminate sulfurous acid gases. Plants will also be required to install the two-stage combustion method and the recycled gas mix method as measures to prevent nitrogenous oxidizing agents and sophisticated collection devices to counter smoke and soot problems. Effective and appropriate methods for sewage treatment will also have to be adopted, including such tertiary treatments as condensation-precipitation, ammonia removal, activated charcoal absorption, sand-filtering, and the like, in addition to such primary and secondary water treatments as fore-treatment, oil separation, neutralization, precipitation, and activated mud treatment. It is also important to select fuels low in sulfurous acid content, such as low-sulfur crude oil, naphtha, and liquefied natural gas (LNG) if we are to eliminate pollution from sulfurous acid gas. We must also hurry with the development of closed-system production processes able to avoid discharging their waste by recovering and recycling it.

While on the subject of pollution policy, I would especially like to stress the use of abundant space and green belts. There should be as much distance as possible between factories within an industrial base and between the industrial base and nearby residential areas. Green belts in these areas can be created using natural or planted groves. Not only will this enhance nature's cleansing capacity and serve both to prevent compound pollution and as rest areas for employees; it is also an indispensable condition for any industrial base as a precautionary measure to save human lives in the event of earthquakes, fires, or other disasters.

In selecting industries for an industrial base, only those applicants which promise to observe the standards should be accepted. Applicants will have to sign binding pollution-prevention agreements with the local governments. After the plants go into operation, they will be under constant surveillance by pollution monitoring and warning systems comprised of measurement instruments and computerized data communication facilities. In this way, it is hoped that not a single person will fall victim to pollution.

While the costs will go up somewhat for an industrial base which achieves such harmony with nature, this cost should, in principle, be borne by the industry as the pollution source. Considering only damage to the corporate image and the indemnification burden that can come from even one victim of pollution, surely it is not possible to invest too heavily in pollution prevention. The OECD Executive Council has also confirmed the "Polluter Pays Principle" (PPP) for pollution costs.

Welfare-Oriented Power Plants

According to MITI estimates, it will take an output capacity of 236 million kilowatts to meet 1985's power demand, more than 3.5 times our capacity as of the end of 1971. Of this, thermal plants are expected to provide half and nuclear plants 30 percent. Yet opposition from local residents has made it difficult for the power companies to expand their present installations or to build new power plants where they had planned.

For this reason, I would like to see power plants built with huge capacities in the large industrial bases and elsewhere, making them energy-supply complexes as well. The Electric Power Development Co., in cooperation with several of the private power companies, can jointly build thermal and atomic

stations to produce power for the vast industrial bases. At the
same time, I would like to see studied the possibilities of building a network of super-high-tension transmission trunk lines
designed to reach consumers throughout the nation. In addition,
it has also been suggested that the power rates in underpopulated areas be lowered in order to help stimulate the inflow of
industries and people and that the taxes on electricity and gas
be changed from local to national taxes, making that revenue
available for distribution on a national basis to facilitate regional development. The idea would be to raise the electricity
and gas taxes for factories and office buildings in overcrowded
areas while exempting the underdeveloped areas from these
taxes and subsidizing local governments for the lost revenue.
I feel that this kind of concept deserves further study.

What can be done to facilitate the location of such vast energy
bases and electrical power plants which does not arouse local
opposition?

The main reason for strong local opposition to the construction of new thermal or atomic plants is the fear of air pollution
or radiation hazards. Opposition also comes from fishermen who
fear that the disposal of cooling water will raise river and sea
temperatures, jeopardizing fishing and raising of seaweed. Additionally, other people stress the point that the construction of
an unsightly power plant will destroy the natural beauty of the
area. Because an electric power plant is largely automated, it
does not contribute significantly to local employment. Besides
that, almost all of the power generated is sent to the big cities.
The net result is that the benefits to the locale are slight and
the residents claim that all they get out of it is pollution.

The first thing to be considered, then, is the absolute guarantee of safety and the complete elimination of pollution. Speci-

fically, this means promoting the development and use of such techniques as desulfurization of heavy oil, smoke desulfurization, gasification desulfurization, etc., in addition to the obviously needed dust collectors as well as equipment for regulating the temperature of cooling water emissions. As to the question of reactor safety, every effort must be made to help residents understand and accept their proven safety on the basis of overseas examples and survey reports from the Safety Deliberation Council. But merely eliminating pollution would be only a passive policy.

We must also consider constructing welfare-oriented power stations or ones which will enhance the welfare of the region and which the local people will gladly accept. For example, heated cooling water can be utilized upon discharge for community-wide heating systems or for heating hot-houses for raising vegetables and flowers or for fish farming. In snowy regions, this could also be used to help clear sidewalks and roads.

Local facilities such as roads, ports, and public meeting halls should also be constructed whenever an electrical power plant is built. It will also be possible to introduce power plants complete with their complement of factories so as to increase the income opportunities for the local area. I would also like to consider "energy parks" to be established along the lines of the industrial parks elaborated upon in the following section. Hasty emphasis upon production alone is bound to be ineffective.

Attractive Industrial Parks

The inland industrial parks of the future will have to be industrial parks in the true sense of the term. With rows of green trees, grassy fields with fountains playing, attractive factory buildings painted in bright yet sedate colors and laid out in an orderly fashion, the overall impression of the industrial park will be, indeed, that of a park. It should also be possible to build parks with one section devoted to such community facilities as restaurants, meeting or recreation centers, gasoline stations, barber shops, post offices, health clinics, and the like. Integrating the industrial park into local life with sporting events at the park's swimming pools, gymnasiums, etc., is also possible.

Still, the factory is a place of production. Even if we build industrial parks, they can hardly be classical parks like Kanazawa's Kenroku-en or Mito's Kairaku-en. As the spearhead for regional development and the heart of the local city formation program, the inland industrial park cannot be an industrial wasteland devoted solely to production facilities. It should be conceived and constructed to provide an environment in harmony with the surroundings where people can work with a genuine sense of well-being.

With its unprecedented economic growth, industrial Japan has become the target of numerous industrial study teams from Southeast Asia and all over the world, and these people have gone away amazed at the sheer size of the Goi, Kashima, or Mizushima coastal industrial belts. Yet when it comes to inland industrial parks, they claim Japan does not have much to show.

Of course, there are inland industrial parks in Japan. Many smaller industrial complexes have been built under the sponsorship of the Japan Housing Corporation, local and municipal governments, and various public corporations. But only a very small number of industrial plants have located in such parks. The vast majority have been built by encroaching upon agricultural land near the big cities in a disorderly jumble along with residential and shopping areas. Most inland industrial location to date has been uncoordinated construction on whatever land was inexpensive enough for industry to buy and build its own factory. It has not been carried out in a systematic way utilizing the pump-priming method to induce comprehensive regional development, including residential areas, shopping areas, green space, agricultural land, or other considerations. Even those industrial parks built with some planning somehow give the impression of lumping manufacturing industries together in one place. Thus the very industries which were supposed to facilitate the construction of attractive neighborhoods seem to have ended up impairing that environment. This is not the way to open the path to the development of new inland industrial parks.

Among the developing nations of Asia, there are several which have learned from the former colonial powers and patterned their development on their superb tradition of city construction. When these nations build industrial zones, the first thing they do is to pave roads and put in sewers. This is followed by developing land, providing homes and service facilities in a neatly arranged fashion. The urban facilities which are located in areas adjacent to Singapore's Jurong Industrial Park even include a zoo and botanical garden. Never in Japan have zoos and botanical gardens been included in the planning of New Industrial Cities or Special Areas for Industrial Consolidation. In Japan, even the means of transportation are given a low priority in building housing complexes or new towns, with the result that they often turn out to be inconvenient "lonely islands on land." There are better new towns built in the Jakarta suburbs than in Japan.

Nevertheless, even in Japan, there have been changes recently in the way factories are built and industrial parks created. There are even some places like Atsugi and Sagamihara in Kanagawa Prefecture which claim to have real industrial parks. The industrial park at Atsugi has used wire-mesh fences surrounding grassy stretches instead of the usual ugly concrete walls around the factories, and coordinated the design of their signs and markings. There are also a number of industrial parks visible from the Tokaido Line which show spacious expanses of grass. The Nagatano Industrial Park built on the former site of an old Imperial Army firing range near the city of Fukuchiyama in Kyoto Prefecture has a total land area of 1,000 acres, including a central park with a natural lake, an apartment complex separate from the industrial area, schools, and service facilities. The Seishin New Town in Kobe has also aimed at the industrial park ideal. Still, we have yet to achieve the kind of true industrial parks seen in the West.

Wide spaces are needed for the industrial parks. In order to obtain them, there ought to be special zoning regulations limiting the size of the building on each lot to set ratios between the area covered by the building and the area of the lot, and between the cubic volume of the building and the area of the lot.

The building-area-to-land-area ratio should be set at 50 percent or less, with building heights and exteriors also regulated and standardized as much as possible. In the West, there are some industrial parks which set this building-area-to-land-area ratio at 20 percent maximum and stipulate that production facilities are to be housed in one-story buildings, with only administrative offices allowed a second story. In order to avoid crowding with buildings, there should also be regulations setting the distances which buildings must be from their site boundaries. There should also be several yards of grass between the building and the road. Employee parking lots, loading areas, and truck and trailer maneuver areas too must all be amply provided for under separate regulations. Permits should be required for advertising and building colors within the industrial park. Plants should be required to install highly effective preventive devices to guard against noxious odors, dust, soot, noise, etc. These regulations can be enforced either by local ordinance or by voluntary agreements by park occupants themselves. The park developer may also incorporate in the contract regulations for site conversion, resale, changes in production methods, or the like.

The problems of management after the industrial park is built are important. No matter how much may have been invested, parks cannot work if the maintenance and operation are badly handled. This question of maintenance covers a wide range of activities, from the maintenance and repair of buildings, greenery, and roads to the cleaning and cooperative disposal of industrial waste. In most countries, this is done by an Industrial Park Operations Committee made up of the participating companies and the developer. In actual practice, it often happens that a joint service company is formed under this Committee's supervision to carry out the actual work of taking care of the site.

Industry grows. Yet the building-land ratio within the industrial park is fixed and the factories soon run up against limits to their expansion. Thus it is necessary for companies locating in such industrial parks to secure ahead of time a certain amount of excess land. By the same token, it may be more appropriate for a factory expecting rapid expansion to locate independently rather than in an industrial park. Yet even if located independently, the industrial park approach should be adopted.

For an inland industrial park, I would estimate about 500 to 750 acres as an appropriate standard scale. By locating small cities of few tens of thousands on the outskirts of a nuclear city of 100,000 to 150,000 people, the industrial parks can be built around these smaller cities. Then I would like to see such small cities grouped into a single larger city of about 250,000 people.

Inducements for Industrial Relocation

Concrete policies to promote the regional dispersion of industry will begin in earnest on October 1, 1972. To this end, I submitted to the 58th Session of the Diet the Industrial Relocation Promotion Bill and the Bill for Reorganization of the Coal-Mining Area Development Corporation into the Industrial Relocation and Coal-Mining Area Development Corporation, and proposed the necessary budgetary, fiscal, and taxation measures for fiscal 1972. The Industrial Relocation Promotion Law incorporates the two major concepts of Departure Promotion Areas for areas which are already overcrowded and should expel some industry, and of Relocation Reception Areas for regions which should attract new industry. Departure Promotion Areas are the existing urban portions of the National Capital Sphere and the Kinki region (with the standing of the Chubu region yet undecided), while Relocation Reception Areas cover a wide range, including all of Hokkaido, Tohoku, Hokuriku, San'in, Shikoku, Kyushu, and Okinawa, as well as a few other prefectures and their adjacent towns and villages.

Five Inducements for Industrial Relocation

There are five major inducements, including loans, subsidies, and tax incentives, for industries moving from Departure Promotion Areas to Relocation Reception Areas.

The first is loans or purchasing in connection with the former site of the relocating industry. It takes an industry some two to three years to acquire a new site to move to, to build a plant there, to install equipment, and then to sell off its old site. The sale of the old site usually provides the greatest source of the company's cash on hand. Yet when the decision is made to move the plant, corporate executives cannot be sure of what price the old site will bring. If they simply sell to another factory, it does nothing to alleviate the overcrowding and to assist industrial dispersion. Accordingly, the Industrial Relocation and Coal-Mining Development Corporation provides loans using the old site as collateral for the period beginning from the time the decision is made to move and ending with the actual sale, with the condition that the old site is not to be sold to another factory. Repayment is made in one lump sum when the site is sold. While there is no limit on the total loan amount available in each case, the maximum collateral value of the site is set at 80 percent of its estimated market value, interest is a low 6.5 percent per annum, and the period of loan is about three years as a rule. It is also permissible to use this loan in combination with a regional development loan or a local dispersion loan from the Japan Development Bank. If a relocating company cannot make an adequate sale of its old site, the Corporation itself purchases the site at current market value and then resells it with the priority orientation toward such public uses as green areas or parks. They can also be sold for public housing or for distribution facilities insofar as that does not have a detrimental effect on the urban environment.

Secondly, the Corporation also makes industrial loans of up to $500,000 per company available at 7 percent per annum for three years to cover such moving costs as equipment disassembly and transport.

Thirdly, the national government provides a subsidy of $16 for every ten square feet of factory floor space to both the relocating industry and to the recepient municipality. This subsidy is to be used for building green belts, parks, pollution-monitoring facilities, nurseries, athletic grounds, gymnasiums, and other facilities to improve relations between the incoming factory and the local community.

Fourth is the accelerated amortization plan permitted for buildings and equipment of factories moving out of Departure Promotion Areas. When a factory moves, it must either scrap or dispose of at nearly scrap prices the buildings and equipment which it cannot take with it. For plant and equipment with many remaining years of depreciation, this can involve a considerable loss. Therefore, a system has been developed whereby the company is allowed to regard the book value of such equipment at the time the decision to move is made as its purchase price, and to depreciate in full the residual value permissible under the Corporate Tax Law until the move is completed, provided that MITI or another competent Ministry approves the relocation plan submitted by the industry. While this system has been used to assist small businesses suffering from the effects of preferential tariffs or wishing to convert their businesses as the result of the "dollar shock" of August, 1971, its appliciation is now extended to large corporations as well in order to promote their factory relocations.

Fifth are the three-year grants provided to compensate in full local governments for taxes lost by exempting incoming plants from the property taxes.

While all legislation pertaining to regional development will apply to new or additional factory construction within Relocation Reception Areas, there are three additional inducements worth mentioning here.

First is a grant to local communities of $16 for every ten square feet of new or additional floor space, to be built within certain limits, which is to be used for environmental conservation and welfare facilities. In effect, the national government provides municipalities in Relocation Reception Areas with construction subsidies for environmental protection and public welfare facilities when a new factory moves in from a Departure Promotion Area, or when new facilities are built or current facilities are expanded without any relation to Departure Promotion Areas.

Secondly, the national government provides interest assistance funds when industrial parks are built by local governments or developmental corporations so that the interest burden does not exceed 6.5 percent per annum.

Third, at the request of the local governments, the Industrial Relocation and Coal-Mining Area Development Corporation initiates, in certain select areas, regional development by actually constructing industrial parks and housing projects to be sold at reasonable prices.

A Punitive Tax for Plants that Stay

A total fund of $50 million has been secured in the general budget and fiscal loan and investment program for fiscal 1972 to support these incentives. Since the actual start of factory relocation promotion policies is scheduled for October, 1972, this six-month budget is equivalent to some $100 million on an annual basis. But the establishment of a special account in the budget will be necessary as it is our plan to sharply increase the funding to $7 or $10 billion by 1985. Assuming the expiration of the corporate tax surcharge (1.75 percent) in March of 1972, I was considering the imposition of an equivalent tax for factories in overcrowded areas as a "Factory Expulsion Tax." The revenue thus generated was to be set aside to fund a special account to promote relocation. However, the extension for another two years of the corporate tax surcharge has made this impractical, at least for fiscal 1972.

Nonetheless, the Factory Expulsion Tax is an effective means for solving the overcrowding problem, and I would definitely like to implement it in fiscal 1973, with the revenue going to a special account for factory relocation. At the same time, I would like to consider special grants to be made to the Relocation Reception municipalities to compensate them for the revenue lost from exempting factories from the property tax. These grants would be a compensatory measure separate from the local grants and available for periods of longer than three years, perhaps for as long as twenty-five years.

While it is debatable whether the Factory Expulsion Tax should be a national tax or a local tax, I feel strongly that this must be a national tax. There will be no alleviation of the regional discrepancies whatsoever if Tokyo or Osaka collect the Factory Expulsion Tax as a local tax and use it in their own areas. This tax can be effective only if the revenue from overcrowded areas is used for inducing industries to local areas. This tax program will be equally beneficial to the great cities troubled by overcrowding.

4

Revamping the Transport Network

Meeting Transport Demands

Development of transport and communication networks as a pump-priming measure is an indispensable prerequisite for promoting industrial relocation and the building of local cities. If it is impossible to move people, goods, and information quickly, accurately, and conveniently in the volumes necessary, it will prove impossible to effect the regional dispersion of production and population. While most local cities and rural villages have the labor force, land, and water needed for production, they do not have the accumulation of social capital which the urban centers have built up over the years. Thus it is necessary to construct roads, railways, and other basic facilities for living and production purposes in order to offset the inconvenience of locating in the countryside.

If effective means of transport are made available, the distance between factory and market need not prove a serious obstacle. Even now, household electrical appliances manufactured in the Kansai region are expanding their sales in Kanto markets, competing favorably with locally produced appliances. By the same token, automobiles manufactured near Tokyo are more than holding their own against local products in the Kansai and Chubu areas. In this sense, the psychological distance and the information gap are obstacles to the regional dispersion of production and population. But this can be solved if we shorten the time-distances between regions by expanding airline services, building nation-wide super-express railways and automobile expressways, and forming national information networks.

At present, a trip from Tokyo to Aomori is usually an overnight affair, but when the new super-express line is completed it will be possible to make the round-trip in a day. The location of a new international airport at Narita to relieve overcongestion at Haneda (Tokyo International Airport) will not inconvenience anyone if the time-distance between Tokyo and the new airport is shortened.

The "General Principles of Urban Policy" has defined the six major directions for providing the basic transport and communications networks as:

1. Building a national network of super-express railways crisscrossing Japan.

2. Systematically constructing a network of automobile roads to connect all four of Japan's main islands with long tunnels and bridges.

3. Constructing international airports capable of coping with the expanding volume of air traffic and with the increasing numbers of super-sonic and jumbo aircraft.

4. Expanding the existing ports for ocean-going vessels and building new international trade ports to meet the expansion in Japan's overseas trade.

5. Formulating a national transportation plan based upon extensive research on the socio-economic costs of transporting different foods over varying distances either by rail, truck, ship, or plane.

6. Creating a basic communications network taking fullest advantage of computers in line with the information revolution, in order to improve the efficiency of our lives and industry.

From the viewpoint of shortening time-distance, the first target must be to bring all major areas of the country within one day's travel. Next will be to reduce the time-distance between Tokyo, Osaka, Nagoya, and other major cities to one hour or less. The third will be to shorten the time-distances between any two points within regions like Tohoku or Hokkaido to the equivalent of time-distances within prefectures.

The construction of super-express railways and automobile expressways has already expanded the one-day travel zone in the Pacific coastal belt from 60 miles to more than 300 miles. This five-fold expansion of the mobility radius means a ten-fold or even fifteen-fold expansion of human activity.

Not only will an expansion of our mobility radius raise production, it will broaden the range of all activities, including consumption, information transmittal, and recreation, enhancing all the functions of our society.

In formulating and implementing a comprehensive traffic system, it is important to consider not only the shortening of time-distances but also the capacity and cost problems of mass-transport. Assuming the advent of a one trillion dollar economy by fiscal 1985, we will be faced with an enormous transport demand which will require the building of more than 5,600 miles of super-express railways, 6,200 miles of automobile expressways, and 4,600 miles of petroleum pipelines, as well as efforts to provide intercoastal shipping ports, make all existing railways double-track and electric, and expand commuter railroads. Consider freight transportation, for example. Even conservative estimates put anticipated demand for freight transportation by 1985 at 820 billion ton-miles, a 4.2-fold increase over fiscal 1969. The ton-mile is a unit for measuring the transportation workload. Ten ton-miles can mean either transporting one ton of goods 10 miles or transporting 10 tons of goods for one mile. Intercoastal shipping, which currently accounts for 42 percent of Japan's total freight movement, can be improved to handle half of the anticipated 820 billion ton-miles. If this is done, overland transport will have to take care of the remaining 410 billion ton-miles. But even the most optimistic estimates of today's rail transport put capacity at no more than 37 billion ton-miles. Therefore, unless railway freight capacity is drastically improved, the remaining 373 billion ton-miles will have to be carried by truck, and this will take a staggering 27 million trucks.

Yet if 27 million trucks were to take to Japan's roads every day, traffic would be virtually paralyzed, even if all long-range plans for road improvement were carried out in full. To put so many trucks on today's congested roads would require regulations to keep two-thirds of all passenger vehicles off. If both all the trucks and all the cars were on the roads, it would cause such a giant traffic jam that 140 billion ton-miles would never get moved. To carry this leftover volume by rail would require a 4.6-fold expansion of today's railroad capacity. To do this would require building more than 5,600 miles of super-express rail lines throughout Japan. This would siphon off much of the present passenger traffic and give the existing lines greater capacity for freight. This means a three-fold expansion of rail freight capacity. In addition, it is also possible to effect another 1.5-fold expansion of capacity by double-tracking and electrifying important railroad lines, quadruple-tracking some especially important lines, and phasing out some stations. The result would be a 4.5-fold increase in rail freight capacity, which, in combination with expanded truck capacity, could be expected to handle a transport volume of almost 410 billion ton-miles.

But that is not the end of the problem. Even if we manage to combine railways and roads and build the capacity to handle this volume, transportation will still be stymied unless we coordinate the flow, volume, and labor force. Accordingly, it is imperative that we coordinate the use of our railways and roadways, defining responsibility for the various modes of transport to exploit their advantages to the fullest. Let us start with the manpower problem. It is presently impossible even to secure the drivers needed to operate 27 million trucks. It is expected that the labor force in 1985 will only be 1.2 times larger than it is today and there will be only 660,000 drivers of commercial trucks, so that, even including teamsters who drive their own trucks, it will be all we can do to secure 1,220,000 drivers.

Based on this calculation, 91 billion ton-miles is the maximum truck transport capacity for 1985. This means we will have to make a determined effort to switch over to air, rail, and inter-coastal shipping, as well as to seriously consider pipelines as the primary means of petroleum transport. In terms of defining areas of responsibility, it seems most reasonable that trucks should handle the short-distance transportation, rails the medium-range tasks, and inter-coastal shipping the long-range needs. Combining all of these factors, it is necessary to give super-express trains the task and the capability of transporting considerable volume of goods as well as people, and to build some 4,600 miles of pipeline to absorb 40 percent or 34 billion ton-miles of the total petroleum transport demand.

Japan's transportation policies have centered upon railways ever since the Meiji Restoration. Yet this is a policy of drawing lines to connect points, and it is this which helped to create the excessive concentration of the great urban centers. What we need now is a transportation policy serving the planes as well as the points, making the points where highways intersect railways, shipping lanes, and air routes the new key points of transportation networks.

The Dawning Super-Express Age

On March 15, 1972, the New San'yo Line was opened for service between Osaka and Okayama. Coupled with the New Tokaido Line already in its eighth year, this has made it possible to travel the 420 miles from Tokyo to Okayama in a mere four hours and ten minutes. If all goes as planned, the entire New San'yo Line will be operational by autumn of 1974 to make it possible for us to travel the 665 miles from Tokyo to Hakata Station (northern Kyushu) in six hours and ten minutes.

There is no need to dwell upon the advantages of the super-express railway here. A passenger boarding the Hikari express out of Tokyo at 8:00 in the morning arrives in Osaka at 11:10 that same morning. With only three hours and ten minutes needed for the one-way trip, it is entirely possible to make a round-trip in a single day. Moreover, the fare is no more than two day's earnings based upon the average national per-capita income.

The super-express railways have also made it very convenient for people in Tokyo and Osaka to visit relatives during the summer or New Year's vacation. By the same token, it has become easier for people to come to Tokyo from rural areas. The fact that super-express trains have carried an aggregate of more than 400 million passengers, the equivalent of four times Japan's population, is eloquent testimony to their convenience.

Between October of 1964 and March of 1971, a total of 363 million passengers took advantage of the New Tokaido Line. One scholar has estimated that these people saved some 835 million hours over what the equivalent travel would have taken them on the old Tokaido Line. In economic terms, this is, in effect, equivalent to $1.8 billion of production. In terms of man-hours saved, it is equivalent to adding some 350,000 white-collar workers to the labor force. A labor force of 350,000 is about the size of the total labor force in the City of Kobe. In such ways, the super-express railways have enabled us to move about more efficiently and have contributed to raising productivity in general.

In addition to the New Tokaido Line which is in operation and the New San'yo Line which is partly completed, plans have already been finalized and work begun on the New Tohoku Line (Tokyo-Morioka), New Joetsu Line (Tokyo-Niigata), and New Narita Line (Tokyo-Narita). Basic planning is also under way on three more lines: the New Hokuriku Line (Tokyo-Toyama-Osaka), New Kyushu Line (Hakata-Kagoshima), and New Tohoku-Hokkaido Line (Morioka-Aomori-Sapporo).

While the New Tokaido and New San'yo Lines were meant to provide a breakthrough in the capacity limits of the old lines, these other lines will serve as pump-priming investments to promote regional development in Hokkaido, Tohoku, Hokuriku, Kyushu, and elsewhere, and to contribute to closing the gap between the Pacific coast and the Japan Sea coast, northern Japan, and southern Kyushu.

However, the construction of such super-express railways does not stop here. Steadily expanding passenger loads indicate that the New Tokaido Line will be unable to carry all of its passengers by 1980, and a second New Tokaido Line will be needed. In addition, there is a long list of other lines needed for regional development, such as the New Ou-Hokuriku Line (Aomori-Akita-Niigata-Toyama-Osaka), New Chugoku-Shikoku Line (Matsue-Okayama-Takamatsu-Kochi), New Kyushu-Shikoku Line (Osaka-Shikoku-Oita-Kumamoto), New San'in Line (Osaka-Tottori-Matsue-Yamaguchi), New Hokkaido Lines (Sapporo-Asahikawa-Wakkanai, Asahikawa-Abashiri, and Sapporo-Kushiro). As these will significantly contribute to regional development, they have the strong support of the local people.

If these more than 5,600 miles of super-express railroads are built crisscrossing Japan, the focal cities will be within one to three hours of each other. For all practical purposes, these focal cities will be unified. Downtown Niigata or Toyama will become as accessible as the suburbs of Tokyo are today. Likewise Matsue will be like a suburb of Kochi, Okayama, or Osaka.

The Ministry of Transport and the Japanese National Railways (JNR) are working on developing a super-super-express railway capable of going 310 miles per hour, twice the speed of today's super-express. With the present system relying upon wheels in traction with rails, there is a physical speed limitation of about 190 miles per hour. Thus a special method called the linear motor has been adopted for the super-super-express. When certain metals are cooled to very low temperatures, they loose much of their resistance to electric current and become highly conductive. This phenomenon is called super-conductivity, and the super-super-express uses the powerful magnetism generated by this super-conductive technique to raise the carriage body up off the railbed. This also cuts down on the "super-express pollution" of noise. When these super-super-express trains are completed, they will be able to make in one day the 2,500-mile round-trip between northern and southern Japan, and it will be possible to take care of business easily anywhere in the country.

Developmental work on the linear motor and super-super-express techniques should be undertaken in earnest as national projects with clearly stated completion targets. I would like to have at least the second New Tokaido Line use this linear motor method.

More than simply connecting heavily populated cities, future super-express railways must be developed as tools for regional development by situating stations in sparsely populated areas and using these stations as foci for development. It is imperative that the JNR and the local governments cooperate in this to acquire land for the new stations and vicinities well in advance. Then this land should be used for the stations, station buildings, squares, bus terminals, and other similar facilities consistant with comprehensive urban planning for the area's development. Also, I would like to consider the establishment of a form of private-public cooperation with private industry joining JNR and local governments in the construction and management of these related facilities. The same approach can

Projected Super-Express Railway Network

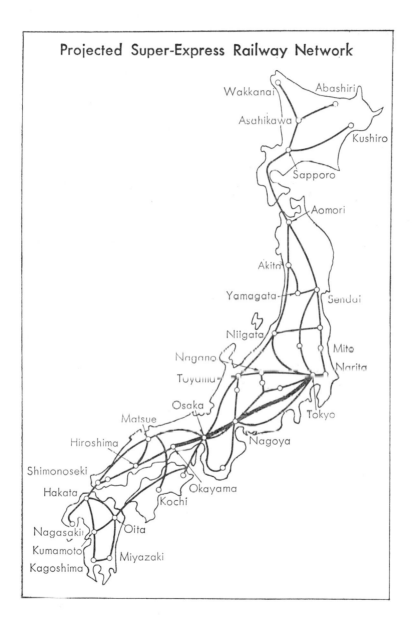

be taken when the Japan Highway Public Corporation builds expressway interchanges and has them serve as the foci for regional development.

In addition to building super-express railways, it is also necessary to improve the capacity on existing lines. For this, about 6,200 miles of existing lines will be double-tracked and electrified, while especially heavily used portions may even require four tracks. The speed of freight trains can also be increased by improving the durability and safety of the rails. Where super-express lines are in operation, most non-commuting passenger traffic can be moved to super-express and the older lines can be used for freight transport. Inter-city freight should, in so far as possible, drop the old method of having freight trains assembled or reassembled at every yard. Instead, freight should be containerized so that goods can be moved to their destinations without delay.

The older lines also have a major role to play for commuting to work and school as well as for freight transport. Again, they serve to connect cities and areas that do not have the benefit of super-express stations with ones that do. It is precisely because the older lines continue to be used for both passengers and freight that the super-express lines, and indeed the entire railway system, can be effective.

One thing which must be mentioned here is the problem of rebuilding the JNR and eliminating deficit lines. The JNR had run up deficits of $2.7 billion by the end of March, 1972, and there has been increasing pressure to abandon those local lines which contribute heavily to this deterioration of the balance sheet.

However, the JNR has an important mission apart from making a profit. It is the JNR which enabled Hokkaido to grow nearly sixty times from a mere 90,000 people in 1872 to its present population of 5,200,000. If all the railroads were making money, we could leave their operation to private enterprise. The same standards as apply to private industry should not be used in discussing the deficits and rebuilding of the JNR.

In the age when urban concentration was accepted, the concept of abandoning deficit local lines had a certain persuasiveness. In an age which seeks comprehensive national development through industrial relocation, the question of local lines should be reassessed in a new light. As is amply illustrated by the history of Hokkaido's development, the leadership role of the JNR in regional development is highly significant. If the abolition of local deficit lines were to result in shutting down industry there, the people would flow to the cities and the disparity between overcrowded urban areas and deserted rural areas would become even worse. This would impose a burden upon the state far greater than the JNR deficits it was intended to eliminate.

If all the local deficit lines in all the areas with heavy snowfall were abandoned and all traffic were switched over to roads, the costs of snow removal alone would be immense indeed. Besides, trucks are often stalled in snowstorms. Comparing roads and railways in the very cold regions, which is really of greater burden on the national economy to maintain? This question deserves careful consideration. Moreover, the deficit generated by local lines running to farming and fishing villages is but one-tenth of the total JNR deficit.

Six Thousand Miles of Highways

If the new super-express railways lead Japan's development along lines, roads make the development of the planes between the lines possible. When most of the people and goods were transported by rail, industry naturally was inseparable from railway stations. With the development of highways and automobiles to facilitate the delivery of goods and people from station to door, or even door to door, it has become easier for industry to be dispersed over wide areas. If there were no roads there would be no residential areas. Japan's railways have a total length of some 12,000 miles, but our roads, including local village streets, run some 600,000 miles.

The Sixth Five-Year Road Construction Plan, begun in fiscal 1970, calls for the investment of $34.5 billion in motorways by the end of 1974. This averages out to more than $6.7 billion per year. When I formulated the three laws which provide the basis for the present Five-Year Road Construction Plan in 1952, the annual expenditures on road construction and maintenance were $67 million. This means that highway investment has been expanded one hundred-fold in nineteen years. By the beginning of the 21st century, we will have to pave about one-fifth of our level land just to cope with the vast road traffic demand.

But let us look at the more immediate demands for 1985. To start with, we should not wait until the target deadline of 1985 to complete the 32 expressways stretching for 4,700 miles decided upon in the National Development Trunk Road Construction Law of 1966 but must complete these within the next ten years and even increase the total to at least 6,000 miles.

Expressways play a major role in the regional dispersion of industry. The town of Ritto in Shiga Prefecture was once an impoverished village without a single factory. With the construction of the Meishin Expressway and the nearby interchange, more than two hundred factories have moved into the area, and transformed the community into a prosperous industrial town. With national Route 1 and Route 8 also converging in this area along with the Meishin Expressway, this has become very advantageous area for industrial location.

The city of Komaki in Aichi Prefecture was formed in 1955 with the consolidation of several villages and towns. Until then it was an agrarian-oriented village with virtually no industry to speak of, with the exception of foodstuffs, clothing, textiles, and related products. The junction of the Meishin and Tomei Expressways and the construction of the Komaki Interchange there have brought this community into the limelight as a production and distribution center.

The completion of the Tomei Expressway has also meant a doubling or tripling of the amount of transport of pork or pigs from Kyushu to Tokyo. A study by the Japan Highway Public Corporation has shown that the four days it used to take to transport piglets from southern Kyushu to Tokyo has been shortened to about one day. Now it is possible to bring them without layover, transporting them from southern Kyushu to Kobe by ferry and then to Tokyo on the Tomei and Meishin Expressways. Thus the piglets do not tire and lose as much weight during the trip and per-truck profits have been raised by $670.

The Osaka fruit and vegetable market is a great trading center as trucks ply the Tomei and Meishin Expressways headed for Osaka with cucumbers from Fukushima Prefecture's Iwase,

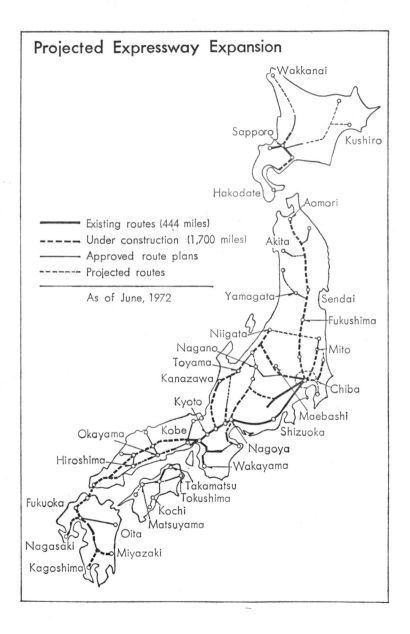

Projected Expressway Expansion

Wakkanai

Sapporo

Kushiro

Hakodate

Aomori

Existing routes (444 miles)
Under construction (1,700 miles)
Approved route plans
Projected routes

As of June, 1972

Akita

Yamagata

Sendai

Fukushima

Niigata

Nagano

Mito

Toyama

Kanazawa

Chiba

Kyoto

Maebashi

Okayama

Kobe

Shizuoka

Hiroshima

Nagoya

Wakayama

Takamatsu
Tokushima

Fukuoka

Kochi

Matsuyama

Oita

Nagasaki

Miyazaki

Kagoshima

green peppers from Ibaraki Prefecture, pears and carrots from Saitama Prefecture, and fruit and vegetables from all over the nation. This is but one more example of how the construction of expressways has expanded the long-distance shipping of perishables. The more expressways that are built, the wider the radius each market embraces and the more competition there is among producing areas. Coupled with trade liberalization, this means, for the economy as a whole, that each area produces what it is best suited for, prices are equalized, and production is rationalized.

Already there are some 440 miles of expressways, often referred to as national development trunk roads, open to traffic if one counts the Tomei, Meishin, Chuo (Fujiyoshida route), and completed portions of the Chugoku, Kinki, Kyushu, and Higashi-Kanto Expressways.

Looking at the advanced industrial nations of the West, we see that America has already opened 31,500 miles and the famous West German autobahns extend for a total length of 2,770 miles. In Italy, there are 2,420 miles of expressways, 1,200 miles in France, and 765 miles in England.

The United States is the world's greatest automobile-owning nation, and we should not expect to catch up when we consider that America has twice our population and twenty-five times our land area. But West Germany, Italy, and England, all of which have smaller populations, less land, and fewer cars than Japan, all surpass Japan in the building of expressways. According to these countries' plans, by 1975, the United States expects to have a total of 41,000 miles, West Germany 4,350 miles, and Italy 4,050 miles. By contrast, Japan expects to have only 1,180 miles of highways completed by that same year. If we ever expect to achieve a European standard of living, it is clear that Japan will have to hurry with the building of expressways.

If the 32 routes and 4,700 miles of expressways being built in Japan are completed, virtually every point in Japan will be conveniently accessible in less than two hours from an expressway.

However, the Tomei Expressway is already overcrowded on holidays, and traffic jams have occurred on parts of the Meishin Expressway. Undoubtedly, it will be necessary in another few years to build a second Tomei Expressway and a second Meishin Expressway.

Loop expressways around large cities at a radius of 20 to 25 miles must still be built. We must also expand the expressways linking the new coastal industrial zones with urban centers and with inland industrial areas, such as the one between northern Kanto's New Ibaraki Port, Mito, Utsunomiya, Takasaki, and Maebashi, to link airports, seaports, and major cities throughout Japan.

We should devote our energies to building lateral roads connecting the Pacific coast with the Japan Sea coast. Given the need to shorten time-distances in a Japan stretching from north to south, so far, of necessity, we have had to concentrate our investment on lengthwise roads. Now, however, we must strengthen our pump-priming investment in lateral roads in order to eliminate the gap between the Pacific coast and the Japan Sea coast and to develop isolated inland rural areas. This is why at least 6,200 miles of expressways will be needed by fiscal 1985.

An ordered road system of 620,000 miles must be established, starting from this expressway framework and including all peripheral roads for everyday use. This requires that functional distinctions be made between roads and new road specifications. For example, the functions of roads may be defined in terms of their specific purposes, such as expressways handling mass, high-speed transport, trunk roads taking care of through traffic, and residential roads for neighborhood use. Again, with the specialization of roads for specific uses such as heavy loads, buses, airport traffic, harbor roads, etc., adequate terminals should be constructed at intersections for passenger stations, freight depots, container exchanges, and the like.

The new road specifications should provide for ten classes of roads, ranging from those with one lane each way plus sidewalks to those with ten lanes each way. Trunk roads should be required to have at least a minimum of three lanes each way, though it is hoped that four or more lanes will become common, with every effort made to promote traffic safety by clearly specifying separate lanes for trucks, buses, passenger automobiles, and passing.

One more type of road specialization is to create recreational roads separate from industrial highways. When the national income has doubled or tripled and the five-day week has become commonplace, it is likely that even more people will use their cars for weekend outings. At present, it takes about one hour from Tokyo to the Shonan beaches (Kanagawa Prefecture) by train. Yet the man taking his family or sweetheart by car faces the grueling prospect of leaving the house early in the morning and not getting back until midnight at the earliest. This is a common story in the summer newspapers. Nevertheless, be it the automobile civilization or the nature of the times, the number of people traveling by car continues to increase. But the fact that industrial traffic and leisure driving converge upon the same roads so that both are delayed in reaching their destinations is hardly desirable for either industry or vacationers. Every year, the number of people spending their vacations away from the city in search of sunshine and green spaces, clean air and blue skies, increases. So we must hurry with the construction of recreational roads to bring our people closer to nature. This requires not only automobile roads but also a very extensive expansion of bicycle paths, forests, and hiking trails to shrines and historic sites.

The important thing for now is that highway policy should distinguish between truck highways and neighborhood roads. Neighborhood roads are those used by people going to and from neighbors' houses, community schools, and local shopping districts. Yet, as things stand now, through-traffic overflow from the trunk roads spills into, and barrels through, these neighborhood roads. It has come to the point that a man cannot even let his guard down in front of his own house. Simultaneously with promoting the construction of by-passes, we must carefully redevelop neighborhood streets in order to solve this problem as soon as possible.

Building and cultivating attractive local towns is an important strategic means for the remaking of Japan. Thus, thought must be given to coordinating and constructing roads for city development and roads to connect farming and fishing villages within each area on a priority basis.

Until now, highway policy has solely emphasized the building of additional highways. From now on we must be concerned with quality. "Highway pollution" problems such as noise, exhaust, and dust must be solved. This in turn requires that we comprehensively plan the use of land for roads and roadsides, allowing for ample landscaping along trunk roads, creating green belts running the length and breadth of Japan.

Linking the Islands: Bridges to Shikoku

There are plans to complete three bridge routes connecting Honshu and Shikoku by fiscal 1985: one between Kobe and Naruto, one between Kojima and Sakaide, and one between Onomichi and Imabari. When completed, the Akashi Strait Bridge connecting Akashi and Naruto will be the world's longest suspension bridge.

These three bridge systems linking Shikoku with Honshu are not being built only for the 3,900,000 people of Shikoku. These bridges are intended to link super-express railroads and expressways; to integrate the Kinki, Chugoku, Shikoku, and Kyushu areas which together total fully one-third of Japan, creating thereby a broader economic sphere. With these bridges, the population of Shikoku, which shrank by 350,000 in the fifteen years between 1955 and 1970, should expand to 6 million and even to 8 million. Given such a return, building bridge systems of this magnitude should not be regarded as extravagant investment.

Seen from the Honshu side, Shikoku seems near and yet far. Even though it is near Kyoto, Osaka, Kobe, to say nothing of Hiroshima and Okayama Prefectures, Shikoku's infrastructure lags behind the rest of the nation, below average in improved roads, double-tracked JNR routes, city water, telephone subscriptions, and many other indices. Although the secondary and tertiary industrial sectors are growing, the per-capita production income was only $1,420 in 1969, as much as 10 percent below the national average. Undeniably, the overall industrial structure is backward. With the completion of these bridges

Projected Bridge Links
Between Honshu and Shikoku

Highway ▬▬▬ Railway ═══

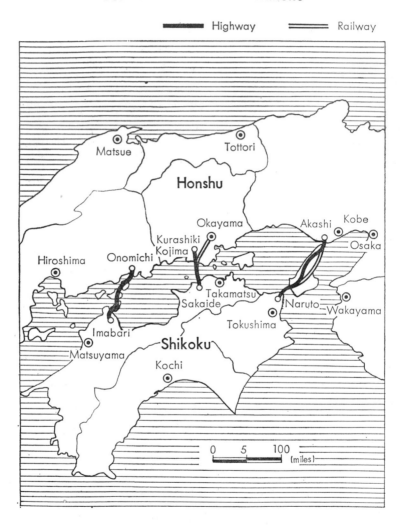

linking Shikoku with Honshu, however, Shikoku's development will be accelerated and the standard of living of the people of the region will rise rapidly.

At present, on the average, about 100,000 people and 170,000 tons of freight are transported between Honshu and the islands of Awaji and Shikoku every day. Passenger vehicles and trucks combined, an average of 17,800 vehicles daily make the journey by ferry. But, because of fog or rough seas, the boats are unable to make the trip as many as sixty days a year.

The congestion of boats in the Inland Sea is appalling. Every day, 1,720 ships pass through the Akashi Straits on an east-west course. This comes to one ship every fifty seconds. Another 180 ships weave their way among them each day on a north-south course.

Despite currents surpassed in rapidity only by those of the Naruto Straits, some 930 ships maneuver their way through the narrow Kurushima Straits every day. Given that these figures are calculated on a 24-hour basis, it is easy to visualize how frantic the rush must be during peak daylight hours. It is indeed a traffic jam surpassing even those in the big cities. These bridges can also contribute to making the Inland Sea safer by providing north-south vehicle routes running over the east-west shipping lanes to create a three-dimensional traffic pattern in the Inland Sea.

Of these three routes, the eastern route between Akashi and Naruto will shorten the time-distance and economic distance between Shikoku and the Kinki region and will point the way to comprehensive development from Osaka Bay to the Kii Channel coast.

Because of the danger of tanker collision, it is unthinkable that giant tankers should be allowed in busy Osaka Bay. It is not even safe to transport pertroleum in small quantities using small tankers. This would only aggravate the already overcrowded situation within the Bay, and an accident could inflict considerable hull damage on a small tanker, with all its accompanying danger of oil spillage. There is no choice but to unload the oil for the Keihanshin (Kyoto-Osaka-Kobe) industrial belt outside of Osaka Bay in areas which are relatively safer from collision. The logical candidate for a petroleum port and storage base is Tachibana Bay which has sea channels navigable by 500,000-ton and one million-ton trans-oceanic tankers. It is also conceivable that a huge man-made island might be built near the Tokushima coast to serve as a petroleum storage base. From these points, the petroleum can be transported to the Keihanshin industrial belt by pipeline installed as a part of the Akashi-Naruto bridge.

The next question is how best to secure the water resources needed for the development of Shikoku. The Yoshino River Comprehensive Development Plan holds the key to this. The Yoshino River runs through central Shikoku. It originates in the Ishizuchi Mountains and flows eastward to Kii Channel near Tokushima City. The total length of this river is 120 miles and its annual water volume is 7 billion tons, boasting the most plentiful water resources in all of western Japan. This vast flow is used to irrigate fields and paddies, provides water for Tokushima, Niihama, Iyo, and Kawanoe, and waters all of Shikoku's four prefectures. In addition, the powerful flow generates electricity at 38 hydroelectric plants situated on the main stream and its tributaries. The Yoshino River is also nicknamed "Rowdy Boy of Shikoku." It got this name because Shikoku is on the regular route for typhoons and is one of the rainiest regions in Japan, making river control extremely difficult.

The Yoshino River Comprehensive Development Plan was

drawn up in 1966. It is expected that the Water Resources Development Corporation will complete construction of the Somyoura Dam by the end of fiscal 1972, which will have a reserve capacity of 310,000,000 tons. In addition, construction has also begun on the Kagawa Irrigation Works, Ikeda Dam, Shinmiya Dam, Old Yoshino Rivermouth Sluice, Yoshino River North Bank Irrigation Works, Kochi Divide, and other sites. The water resources newly generated by these projects can be piped from Tokushima for municipal and irrigation water for the coastal region along Tachibana Bay, the Toyo New Industrial City along the Inland Sea, and the Sanuki Plain, as well as for Kochi Prefecture's Pacific coast. If the 4,800 small reservoirs in the Sanuki Plain should thus become superfluous, it would be possible to put them to more sophisticated uses for land development. Moreover, if a water surplus develops on Shikoku, this could, with the consent of the people of Shikoku, be sent by pipe across the Akashi-Naruto Bridge to provide water to the Hanshin (Osaka-Kobe) area via Awaji Island.

Under the Lake Biwa Comprehensive Development Plan, water is to be taken from Lake Biwa at a rate of forty tons per second to compensate for the inadequacy of the Yodo River in meeting the overwhelming demand for water. Accordingly, it is possible that the level of the lake may drop an additional 5 feet during a draught, which would mean that the shoreline would recede more than 1,600 feet along the east bank's shoal. Inclusion of water and petroleum pipes on the connecting bridge would also contribute to covering the costs of its construction.

It is also reasonable for the Akashi-Naruto Bridge to accommodate railway tracks going from Tokushima along Cape Sata, through the undersea tunnel to Oita, and linking the New Shikoku-Kyushu Line with the New Tokaido Line and the New San'yo Line. The Shikoku Cross-Country Road will be linked with the San'yo Highway, Meishin Expressway, and Tomei Expressway. With this system of super-express railways and expressways, Shikoku will be brought closer not only to the Kinki sphere but to the Nagoya and Tokyo economic spheres as well. The development of Awaji Island will also be accelerated. Shikoku's Muroto-Anan-Coast Quasi-National Park is famous for its tropical plants and sea turtles. If a connecting bridge is built, people will be able to come from Kyoto, Osaka, and Kobe, and even Nagoya and Tokyo, to see the sights and swim in the ocean, developing the area as a giant resort area.

I would also like to see built a New Chugoku-Shikoku Line linking Matsue, Okayama, Sakaide, and Kochi on the middle of the three sets of Shikoku-Honshu connecting bridges, between Kojima and Sakaide. Divided by the three natural barriers of the Chugoku Mountain Range, Inland Sea, and Shikoku Mountain Range, this area has traditionally been divided into four distinct economic spheres. Of the four, the San'in area and the area south of the Shikoku Mountain Range have been economically backward. By running the Chugoku-Shikoku lateral highway and the super-express railway along the Kojima-Naruto route, it will be possible to connect these four isolated economies and to embark upon new development.

Historically, Sanuki has been the front door to Shikoku. Even during the Edo Period, pilgrims traveling to the Kompira Shrine, then the second-most heavily visited holy place after the Ise Shrine, passed by way of Marugame and Tadotsu. Since the opening of the Uno-Takamatsu JNR ferry service, this has been replaced by Takamatsu. At present, the four ports of Takamatsu, Sakaide, Marugame, and Tadotsu handle between 60 and 70 percent of all automobiles arriving in Shikoku by ferry. Thus it is only natural that one of the bridges connecting Shikoku with Honshu should be here.

This bridge may also serve to connect the industrial belt on the Okayama Prefecture side, including Okayama, Kurashiki, Mizushima, and Tamashima, with the industrial belt running from Takamatsu to Sakaide, Kawanoe, Iyo-Mishima, and Niihama. We should also consider extending one branch of the petroleum pipeline from Tachibana Bay on the Akashi-Naruto route to run along the Inland Sea coast in Kagawa Prefecture and then using it to transport oil across the Kojima-Sakaide Bridge to the Okayama side.

The Onomichi-Imabari route, westernmost of the three, differs from the other two in that it will be a vehicle route without any provision made for railway tracks. While there are numerous advantages to this route to be noted, I would like first to touch upon its relation to the Sukumo and Nagahama regions which have great development potentials.

Along with Mutsu, Tachibana, and Shibushi, Sukumo Bay is one of Japan's few natural harbors with a depth sufficient to allow large tankers of over 500,000 tons to enter. In the past, it also included Shikoku's largest shipbuilding yard and the rest port of the Imperial Navy's Combined Fleet, but these have completely disappeared now. I would like to utilize this good port for oil from overseas and as a medium-scale industrial base. Standing as it does at a critical crossroads for traffic across the Kojima-Sakaide route through Kochi and Suzaki and for traffic across the Onomichi-Imabari route through Nagahama, Yahatahama, Uwajima, and Sukumo, it has great development potential and can be developed upon the twin pillars of Sukumo Bay's industry and Ashizuri Quasi-National Park's tourism.

The Port of Nagahama has excellent natural conditions as an industrial port, and it will also be possible to secure city and industrial water by exploiting the resources of the Hiji River to develop the area as an industrial center. While the Nagahama coastal industrial belt is already moving toward development, I think it would also be feasible to lay an oil pipeline from Sukumo Bay and Nagahama Port across the Onomichi-Imabari Bridge to transport oil to Hiroshima and Yamaguchi Prefectures.

It will also be possible in the future to install a petroleum pipeline in the undersea tunnel between Cape Sata and Saganoseki when the Kyushu-Shikoku super-express railway is built. By linking Chugoku with western Shikoku and with the Onomichi-Imabari route, then connecting Kyushu and Shikoku with a super-express railway line, and, if necessary, locating oil and water pipelines along both of these routes, we can complete a freight and passenger transport loop road from Akinada and Suonada through Bungo Channel to further develop the western Inland Sea. Laying a pipeline across the Onomichi-Imabari vehicle bridge will make it possible to supply water to isolated Inland Sea islands such as Oshima and Omishima and thus to meet the increased water demand that expanded tourism may be expected to generate.

In this way, the Honshu-Shikoku connecting bridges will create a functional integration of the four economic spheres of Kinki, Chugoku, Shikoku, and Kyushu and will make possible broad regional development. My emphasis that "Shikoku can become the gateway to Japan" is by no means an empty exaggeration.

Port and Harbor Development

The development of a maritime nation such as Japan cannot be discussed without reference to its ports and harbors. Since the bold decision of the Meiji Government to make Japan a modern nation, Japan has moved steadfastly to expand and strengthen the nation to stand equal with the Great Powers of the West and, since shortly after the Meiji Restoration, has devoted its energies to building railways and ports. Specifically, a vast amount of government funds were invested in building and renovating Kobe and Yokohama as Japan's windows to the world.

As a port for the raw cotton import trade, Kobe served as a central supply base for the Hanshin and Chukyo (Nagoya and vicinity) spinning industries while Yokohama was active as a port for exporting the silk products of the Kanto region. Warehouses, commerce, and light industry flourished in these port towns, and soon they became full fledged international trading ports for liners plying the sea lanes of the world. Following Kobe and Yokohama, Kanmon (Shimonoseki-Moji), Osaka, Nagoya, Shimizu, and, much later, Tokyo, were also developed into international trading ports.

At the same time, apart from these trading ports, industrial ports were built to import coal, iron ore, timber, and other natural resources and to export finished products. Dokai Bay and Muroran were among first of these ports.

Industrial Ports

Locating industries on coasts was one of the major factors which enabled resource-poor Japan to succeed in the fierce postwar international competition and claim a place as one of the world's advanced industrial nations. In Europe and America, which have their own resources, heavy and chemical industries developed in inland areas where raw materials from mineral and coal mines were easily available. This eventually resulted in creating a big burden in overland transport costs. By contrast, Japan, importing virtually all of its main natural resources from overseas, sought to lower transport costs by selecting for its heavy and chemical industries sites where ports could be constructed. Taking petroleum for example, Japan brings 92 percent of its total imports from the Middle East sources which are more than 5,000 miles away. However, with 300,000-ton tankers, the transportation costs come to about $3.30 per ton of petroleum. This is about the same as the domestic shipping costs between Tokyo Bay and the Inland Sea. Thanks to the use of giant tankers, it is just as if Japan had the world's largest oil field within its own borders. The same conditions pertain to other industries such as iron and steel, aluminum smelting, and electric power.

Natural conditions required for building ports and harbors are deep water and protection from the open sea. Today, with the development of dredging techniques, it has become possible to dredge channels even in shallow water and to use the fill to reclaim land for new industrial sites. The conditions for building a coastal industrial zone are a level hinterland, plentiful water, a large population and readily available labor force, and a sufficiently developed consumer market. This way, all necessary resources, labor, market, and industry are located in the same region. It is in this sense that Tokyo Bay and Osaka Bay have few equals anywhere in the world as suitable locations for coastal industrial zones. It is only natural that Japan's industrial production should be concentrated on the coast around Tokyo and

Osaka Bays. Before the War, the two ports of Amagasaki and Kawasaki were the major industrial ports in these bays. After the War, the construction of Kawasaki Steel's giant works in Chiba along the Tokyo Bay shore stimulated other heavy and chemical industries which rapidly developed in Wakayama and Sakai along Osaka Bay, Mizushima and Harima along the Inland Sea, and Oita and elsewhere along Beppu Bay.

Progress in port and harbor technology made it possible to excavate and construct industrial ports even in rough ocean outside of the bays. The feasibility of this technology was confirmed with the construction of Kashima Port, now capable of handling cargo vessels of the 200,000-ton class. The building of Kashima Port was based on technology developed while constructing Tagonoura Port, Ishinomaki New Port, Tomakomai Port, and others. And the success of this port testifies to the technical feasibility of building a second Kawasaki Port or Amagasaki Port in the open sea.

The internationalization of the Japanese economy has brought about an increase in the volume of ocean transport, and in all likelihood ship sizes will continue to grow in order to handle this vast cargo more efficiently. The 370,000-ton Nisseki Maru was launched in April of 1971. And the Japanese ship-building industry has already received orders from England for two 470,000-deadweight-ton tankers. Before those orders were received, the Minister of Transport in July of 1970 had inquired about the possiblity of developing techniques for building a 1,000,000-deadweight-ton tanker, which is said to be already technically feasible. This signals the dawning of the age of the super-tanker. At the same time, ore carriers, LNG-carriers, and others are becoming increasingly larger and specialized.

Concurrent with this, overcrowding developed not only in the coastal industrial zones along Tokyo and Osaka Bays but also in seagoing traffic there. It is impossible to expect the existing ports to perform any more than their present role. In the future, we must construct large-scale industrial ports in outlying areas capable of accepting the vast volumes needed of such natural resources as petroleum, iron ore, non-ferrous metal ores, coal, timber, and natural gas. In building the large-scale industrial bases planned for eastern Tomakomai, Mutsu-Ogawara, Akita Bay, Suo-Nada, and Shibushi, it is also imperative that we simultaneously construct appropriately scaled industrial ports.

Assuming that Japan's 1985 demand for petroleum will reach 700,000,000 tons per year, it will be necessary for the Japanese ports to handle a total of 1,400 entries by 500,000-ton tankers annually. This comes to 3.8 fully loaded 500,000-ton tankers calling at Japanese ports every day. A fully loaded 500,000-ton tanker requires a water depth of approximately 100 feet when it is riding lowest. This means that ports will have to have at least a depth of 115 to 130 feet to allow some margin for maneuvering within the port. Of all Japanese ports, only Mutsu, Tachibana, Sukumo, and Shibushi meet this requirement. All four had been used by the old Imperial Navy for its Combined Fleet. These are among the few good natural harbors available in Japan, and are the best-suited candidates for industrial or distribution ports.

Of course, not all of the tankers of the future will be of the 500,000- or one million-ton class. Even if the supertankers cannot enter a port directly, it will always be possible to construct sea berths within the bay and pump out petroleum from tankers anchored there. With regard to the construction of petroleum storage and transit bases in conjunction with petroleum ports, the more feasible candidate locations in terms of natural conditions include Funka Bay (Hokkaido), Yamada Bay (Iwate Prefecture), Ishinomaki Bay (Miyagi Prefecture), Hirota (Iwate Prefecture), Nanao Bay (Ishikawa Prefecture), Tateyama (Chiba Prefecture), Shizuura Bay (Shizuoka Prefecture), Ise Bay (Mie Prefecture), Yura (Ehime Prefecture), Yuya Bay (Yamaguchi Prefecture), Beppu Bay (Oita Prefecture), Imari Bay (Saga Prefecture), Sakito (Nagasaki Prefecture), and Kin Bay (Okinawa Prefecture).

International Trading Ports

With the dispersion of industry, we must also accelerate the development of new international trade ports. While the Ministry of Transport has designated Kobe, Yokohama, and fifteen other ports of special economic significance as Specific Important Ports, a look at this list shows that they are mostly near Japan's three largest cities, with fully eleven around the National Capital sphere, Chubu region, and Kinki region. Figures for fiscal 1969 show that 87 percent of all export cargoes were handled by the nine ports of Tokyo, Yokohama, Shimizu, Nagoya, Yokkaichi, Osaka, Kobe, Shimonoseki, and Kita-Kyushu.

This concentration comes from liners striving for fast service congregating at the ports with the best cargo-handling facilities in order to load and unload their cargoes quickly. With the advent of container ships, prompt and large-volume movement has become possible. It is not uncommon to find ships shuttling between two ports at speeds of about 25 knots. Thus the ports of call for container ships are limited to the big-city ports such as Tokyo, Yokohama, Osaka, Kobe, Nagoya, and Yokkaichi with their superior cargo-handling capacities. So it often happens that export cargo, first loaded in Hokkaido or Tohoku, is shipped to

Yokohama or one of the other major ports for reloading on liners or container ships.

However, industrial relocation will serve as an impetus to local development so that Hokkaido, Tohoku, Hokuriku, San'in, Shikoku, Kyushu, and other regions will develop into more viable economic entities. We should provide the regional focal ports with loading facilities and build them into international trade ports so that liners can call there. This will help alleviate the immobilizing congestion at the present big-city ports, and at the same time it will contribute to the creation of urban functions and the regional development of these areas. As for the Japan Sea, the Port of Vrangel is being constructed through Soviet-Japanese cooperation. With further progress in Soviet-Japanese relations it may become feasible to link Niigata and Vrangel Ports with liner service and even to use the trans-Siberian railroad to ship goods overland as far as Europe. If Japanese super-express railway technology can be applied to the Siberian railroad, it will be possible to shorten considerably the sea and land transportation time between Niigata, Moscow, and Europe.

Distribution Ports and Pipelines

Along with trade ports and industrial ports, the construction and improvement of distribution ports will be indispensable in the future. We must make a special effort to improve ports for ferries to meet the expansion of domestic ferry transport. It is forecast that the present waterborne cargo movement of about 400 million tons in the Port of Tokyo will increase to 1,200 million tons by 1985. In order to avoid congestion in the Port of Tokyo, we should build a new northern Kanto port in Ibaraki from which to send goods to the Keihin (Tokyo-Yokohama), Keiyo (Tokyo-Chiba), and inland Kanto regions by railroads,

Petroleum Pipeline Master Plan and Proposed Central Terminal Stations (CTS)

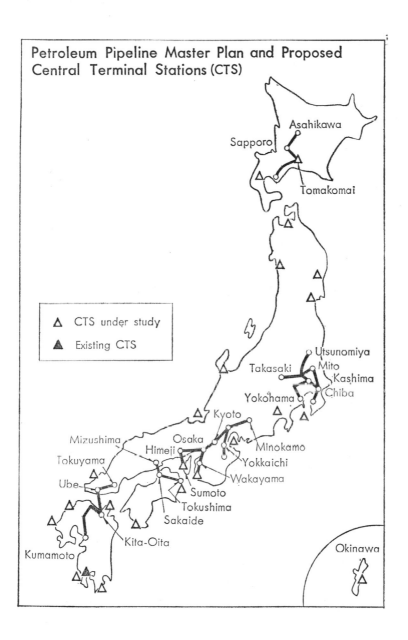

expressway, and pipelines. The same thing should be done for Osaka Bay and the Inland Sea.

Considering petroleum transport in relation to these distribution ports, most of the intermediate-range transport of oil from the storage and transit bases should be done by pipeline. Pipeline transport of petroleum eliminates those traffic problems caused by oil trucks, saves labor, and lowers distribution costs. According to a study by the Ministry of Transport, setting intercoastal tanker transport costs for a distance of 60 miles as a base unit of one, the cost by pipeline is two, that by railway tank car is four, and that by truck is 20. While it only takes six people to transport 10,000 tons of petroleum daily by pipeline, this requires 1,300 people by truck. Moreover, the trucks cannot even begin to compete with pipelines in terms of physical capacity.

At present, there are only about 600 miles of petroleum pipelines in Japan, most of them between factories within complexes. In the United States, on the other hand, pipeline operations are already well established. By 1969 a total of 142,000 miles of pipelines was carrying both crude oil and petroleum products, while Europe had 9,300 miles of pipelines. The United States and West Germany are said to rely upon pipelines for approximately 45 percent of all petroleum distribution.

Against this background, the Government submitted the Bill Concerning Petroleum Pipeline Projects to the 68th regular session of the Diet. Beside encouraging the pipeline industry, this bill was also designed to provide for the supervision of transport safety. Already, the Airport Corporation Pipeline (running 28 miles from the Port of Chiba to the Narita Airport) is being constructed by the New Tokyo International Airport Corporation, and is due to be completed in early 1974. Next planned for construction are the JNR pipelines being laid within the railway rights-of-way (70 miles between Kawasaki, Yokohama, Hachioji, and southern Saitama) and the Kanto pipelines being built with joint private capital (178 miles between Chiba, Saitama, Takasaki, and Utsunomiya). Plans are also being studied to build a 156-mile petroleum pipeline in Hokkaido linking Muroran, Tomakomai, Sapporo, and Asahikawa. By 1985, I would like to see at least 40 percent of all petroleum transport in Japan done by pipelines.

There are considerable numbers of people who fear that petroleum pipelines would pose grave dangers in case of earthquakes. However, recent progress in pipeline materials and welding technology have made pipelines extremely resistant to earthquakes. This has already been proved by the Niigata and Los Angeles earthquakes. Also, since petroleum, unlike gas, is not piped under pressure, there is little danger of explosion even if a pipeline should rupture.

According to data compiled by the OECD Petroleum Committee, the chance of a fatal accident with an oil pipeline is about fourteen hundred times less than with trucks. Still, every priority should be given to ensuring the highest safety standards in laying and operating petroleum pipelines.

Dam Construction for Water Needs

Man cannot live without water. The ancient civilizations all developed along rivers and watersheds, and the questions of flood control and irrigation have long been major political tasks. For the Japanese people, who are rice planters utilizing wet paddies, nature's bounty of pure water is indeed the very staff of life.

The industrial development which was the driving force in building Japan into a modern nation after the Meiji Restoration was supported by plentiful water resources, just as the postwar economic recovery has been greatly helped by hydroelectric power and other uses of water.

Average annual precipitation in Japan is 72 inches, or a total volume of 670 billion tons. Of this, subtracting that part which is lost into the soil or otherwise, the remaining 520 billion tons of water flows into streams and rivers. Compared with the average rainfall for all nations of 29 inches, Japan has 2.5 times as much rain and may be said to be a nation blessed with abundant rain. Yet, if one divides rainfall by population, Japan has only 6,600 tons per person, or less than one-fifth of the comparable figures for the United States and the Soviet Union. Moreover, most of Japan's rivers are fast-flowing and much of that precious water rushes unchecked to the sea. If we are to utilize fully the water which nature provides, it is first necessary to trap this water. But many of the sites appropriate to building reservoirs have already been dammed, and any new dams built will necessarily be inefficient and costly as reservoirs.

In the National Capital Sphere, for example, there are now 17 dams under construction or completed, and the development costs under two cents per ton of water. However, the cost of dams now being planned will be between two and seven cents, and the cost per ton for the 25 dams planned for development after that will rise above seven cents.

Demand for water increases unceasingly. According to a MITI study, total water volume used by industries in 1970 was 98 million tons per day, or 36 billion tons for the year as a whole. Since half of this was water recovered and recycled by factories, the actual river or underground water resources used were 18

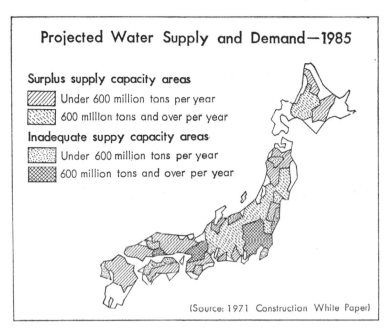

Projected Water Supply and Demand—1985

Surplus supply capacity areas

▨ Under 600 million tons per year

▩ 600 million tons and over per year

Inadequate suppy capacity areas

▢ Under 600 million tons per year

▨ 600 million tons and over per year

(Source: 1971 Construction White Paper)

billion tons per year. Adding to this the 53,400 million tons of water used by agriculture and the 9,200 million tons for home use, Japan's total demand is 80,600 million tons a year. If all of this is to be obtained from run-off, there must be a 16 percent utility rate for our streams and rivers.

What will the demand for water be like in 1985? Forecasts by MITI predict that industrial demand will increase more than three-fold over 1970 to 320 million tons daily. Even if we subtract that part which can be recovered and used again, we will need 57 billion tons of water every year for industrial uses alone. Even if the demand for agricultural water remains constant at 54 billion tons, home-use demand is expected to go up to 20,400 million tons per year, so that the total water supply will have to be some 131,400 million tons. If rivers and streams are relied upon to provide all of this water, their utilization rate must jump to 25 percent by 1985. Taking into account water reserves absolutely necessary if water quality is to be maintained and our rivers are to be habitable for fish, the utilization rate of actually available river water must be as high as 35 to 40 percent.

While it is the policy of MITI to raise the recovery and recycling rate for industrial water to 70 percent in order to save water, industrial water demand will still reach 34,200 million tons annually by 1985, and the total demand, including agricultural and home water uses as well, will reach 108,600 million tons. In this case, river utilization will be 21 percent. But that is not the end of the problem. It is possible to raise the river utilization rate to meet the 1985 national water demand. The problem is with regional water shortages, especially the serious shortages anticipated for the overcrowded Kanto and Kinki areas.

According to regional water use data put together by the Ministry of Construction in April of 1971, the total water demand in 1985 for the Keihin and Keiyo regions will be approximately 7,200 million tons per year.

Supply capability, on the other hand, will be only about 4,100 million tons, mainly from the Tone River but also from the Ara River, rivers within Chiba Prefecture, and the Sagami and Sakawa Rivers in Kanagawa Prefecture. Simple subtraction leaves a vast annual deficit of some 3,100 million tons. At the same time, the Keihanshin (Kyoto-Osaka-Kobe) region will have an annual demand of 4,140 million tons in 1985 to be met from a supply of only 2,200 million tons, primarily the 2,060 million tons from the Yodo River but also including water taken from the Kino River, Muko River, and Yamato River. This means a deficit of some 1,940 million tons. Unless something is done, Tokyo and Osaka will suffer from very severe water shortages in a few years.

Yet how are we to secure the needed water resources? One way is to rationalize industrial water uses. Recycling and multiple-use of industrial water is possible, and the recovery rate in this area of striking demand growth should be raised to 70 percent.

Second is the wide-area use of water with the understanding and consent of local residents. Already the Ministry of Construction has embarked upon rechanneling operations to divert water from the Kinu River and from Lake Kasumigaura into the Tone and Ara Rivers which flow into the Keiyo (Tokyo-Chiba) region. It may also be feasible to direct water into the Kanto region from the Shinano River, Tone River, and Fuji River to the west. In the Kinki area, water diversion is also possible from the Kino River, Shingu River, Yura River, and others. However, the dispersion of production and population from areas of intense water demand and overcrowding to areas with the potential for future development is also of fundamental importance in connection with the development of water resources In order to meet the immense demand for water in 1985, we must develop our water resources based upon national planning done well in advance. Besides building multi-purpose-dams at the headwaters of our major rivers, sluices and river lakes must also be constructed further downstream near the rivermouths to create new resources.

This means building not only large-scale strategic dams but also the smaller local dams necessary to meet local needs. Together, more than 1,100 dams will have to be built throughout Japan by 1985. Since there are presently 205 dams supplying industrial and home-use water, quite apart from those for agricultural purposes, we will have to build more than five times that number. Along with the development of water resources, the task of providing drinking water systems for homes and factory water delivery systems in tune with urban and industrial location planning also requires prompt attention.

Again, as well as making every effort to supply homes with high-quality water from reservoirs and to have factories make the fullest possible use of water recovered within their own processes, it is necessary to develop new, unconventional sources of water. MITI has a model plant under development capable of recycling sewerage and industrial effluent through sophisticated treatment which proves the technical feasibility of recovering water of remarkably high purity. At about 10 cents per ton per day, costs are still above those from standard sources, but hopefully costs will go down as the scale of production goes up. This technology is also an effective way of dealing with environmental questions by building closed systems for water use.

The desalination of sea water is being researched by the Agency of Industrial Science and Technology. Although costs are still rather high at 40 cents per ton per day, the goal is to reduce this to 13 cents by 1975. In this way, in addition to relying upon rivers and dams, we must also work to apply modern science to creating new sources of water.

At the same time, the question of flood control is just as important now as it always has been. The 1959 Ise Bay Typhoon claimed a record toll of 5,000 deaths and $1.7 billion in direct damage. Sparked by this devastation, work was stepped up on reinforcing and controlling major streams and rivers. However, recently there has been conspicuous flooding and landslide damage from smaller rivers and steams in urban areas on which work has been somewhat neglected.

As general flood control measures, there are a number of steps which should be taken, including conservation of the forested areas which store our water; building dykes for flood-control and embankments to limit sand encroachment; renovating dams through the removal of accumulated silt; rejuvenating rivers, including the clearing of river channels and river beds; and improving of effluent outlets and sluice embankments. It goes without saying that flood control is intimately related to national planning and urban redevelopment. One of the first needs is to halt the land subsidence in the industrialized sections of our major cities. Not only does this invite flood damage; it also affects buildings, roads, and bridge safety. It is also very difficult to restore an area once it has subsided. Accordingly, we must hurry with the building of industrial water delivery systems and begin to move toward a total ban on the pumping of underground water, since it is that pumping which causes this land subsidence.

Regarding water, I would also like to emphasize here the importance of preventing water pollution. We must not forget that water is the very fountain of life. While strict pollution-prevention controls should obviously be applied to industrial effluents, I would also like to see greater purification of residential waste water with chemical techniques. Unless the Sumida River and Yodo River are purified to the point that people can enjoy fishing at their mouths, we cannot truly be said to have accomplished our task of remodeling the Japanese archipelago.

The Sky Is the Limit

The oceans and the skies offer the only routes to link Japan with the world. The jet age which opened in the decade of the 1960's not only made air travel faster but also made it even safer and more comfortable. In the 1970's, the appearance of Jumbo 747's has made mass transport by air possible and overseas travel even more convenient. As a result, air travel has established itself as the decisively dominant form of international travel and now accounts for 90 percent of the total.

Reflecting the heightened activity in international traffic for trade and tourism, there has been a conspicuous increase in the number of travelers using international airlines flying into and out of Japan. The total number of both Japanese and foreign passengers in 1970 was 3,280,000, a 23.5-fold increase over the last fifteen years. During this period, the average annual rate of growth has been 22.5 percent, well above international standards. Looking ahead to 1985, most experts agree in predicting that passenger traffic on international carriers will pass even the 40,000,000 mark. This is a twelve- to thirteen-fold increase over current figures. It is expected that air cargo transport too will expand sharply. In 1970, 67,000 tons of air cargo were sent overseas from Japan while 43,000 tons were brought into Japan, making a total of 110,000 tons transported by air. In 1985, however, the combined inbound-outbound total will be at least 3 million tons, and there is a strong possibility that this may go as high as 5 million tons. This maximum figure of 5 million tons is forty-five times the comparable 1970 figure, and even the lower 3 million ton figure is an increase of twenty-seven times.

It is impossible to handle 40 million international passengers and more than 3 million tons of cargo at the Haneda International Airport alone. Thus, in addition to the New Tokyo International Airport under construction at Narita, careful consideration is also being given to possible sites for a new international airport near Osaka. Here I would like to make note of only two of the many points to be considered in future airport planning in connection with industrial relocation.

One of these has to do with the construction of new international cargo airports. As well as serving as *entrepot* for international cargoes linked with domestic air-freight and land transport, I would like to think of these airports as being integrated with the building of new industrial locations, the "airport-adjacent industrial areas" concentrating on such knowledge-intensive industries as electronics, precision machinery, and so forth. In addition to such traditional air-freight cargoes as mail, film, newspapers, magazines, books, jewelry, etc., there has been an increase recently in shipments of industrial products such as television sets and tape-recorders and raw materials such as nuclear fuels. As the Japanese industrial structure becomes more knowledge-intensive, it is certain that there will be an increase in the number of compact and high-value-added products that can be profitably sold even with slightly higher transport fares. Along with information gathering, speed in innovation and transportation of parts and products will become decisive in coping with the rapid changes in the world market and for surviving international competition. The introduction of larger aircraft and lowering of air-freight rates will vastly expand the range of products carried by air. In the future, air cargo transport will likely play a role equal to that of liners and container ships.

If the international division of labor continues to progress, it is conceivable that it may develop into a system whereby products from all over the world, including components and units from the developing nations for example, will be flown into Japan in containers to be assembled here. And of course components and assembly units made in Japan may be shipped all over the world by air container. There is no doubt that air transport will increase not only for such components and units but also for finished products such as computers, peripheral equipment, business machines, medical equipment, optical equipment, measuring instruments, etc.

Since these knowledge-intensive industries require highly technical skills, it is impossible to locate them far from the big cities. Consequently, it is areas along the Pacific coast, specifically along the Ise Bay and the Suruga Bay, which are the likeliest locations for these international freight airports and airport-adjacent industrial areas. However, I do not think there is any need to restrict our search for suitable sites to existing urban concentrations alone. If the comprehensive national development plan makes it possible to build a nation-wide network of transportation and communication facilities which is as good as anything the big cities have to offer, then the Tohoku or southern Kyushu areas where the necessary land is readily available can be superior sites.

The second point to be noted in considering airport construction in relation to future industrial relocation is the improvement of local airports. By 1985, some 120 million passengers will be using domestic airline service, which will mean a total of 240 million airport boardings and disembarkations per year. Air travel will also become more popular as personal income and leisure increase, and people will travel more by air on long trips. Recreational flying will also increase. In Japan, it is logical to develop the short take-off and landing (STOL) aircraft which do not require long runways or extensive airport facilities to link local centers with each other and with urban centers. Along with this, I would also like to consider locating airport-adjacent industrial sites in connection with the development of local airports.

PART III

*Urban Remodeling
and Regional Development*

5

Toward More Livable Cities

Cities: Information Nerve Centers

Political, economic, social, cultural, and many other functions of Japanese life are concentrated in major metropolitan areas such as Osaka, Nagoya, and, most notably, Tokyo. Of these functions, those which constitute the nerve center of society are the ones most conspicuously concentrated in big cities. Politically, Tokyo is the center of legislative and executive power, as symbolized by the Diet building and the cluster of government offices to house Finance, MITI, Construction, and other Ministries. This is also the case for business. Most of the nation's leading corporations capitalized at $17 million or more have their headquarters in Tokyo, including Nippon Steel, Nissan Motors, Mitsui & Company, and Fuji Bank. The Bank of Japan—the bank of banks—also has its head offices in Tokyo.

Many universities, research organizations, newspaper companies, publishing houses, and printing firms are congregated in large cities, indicating an extraordinary concentration of nerve-center functions in the areas of education, research, and culture. In addition to being nerve centers, the big Japanese cities are the primary centers of both production and distribution activities with their numerous manufacturing plants, wholesalers, retailers, and warehouses. A disorderly mixture of these functions with recreational facilities and masses of dwellings—this is the Japanese metropolis of today.

Such functional concentration, particularly of nerve centers, in big cities makes it almost impossible for people in outlying areas to work without some ties to them. Local cities, deficient in urban functions, tend to become subordinate to the big cities and uniformly lacking in individuality and attractiveness.

In a way, all Japanese cities today are, in varying degrees, like the physically handicapped, be they big cities like Tokyo and Osaka or smaller cities in the country. The large cities are suffering from "hypertrophy" caused by the overconcentration of both people and activities and the "arteriosclerosis" of congested traffic. This is further complicated, literally, by asthma caused by the fumes from industrial plants and the exhaust from automobiles.

Like a human body without a brain, local cities have many of the same production facilities and shopping centers but lack their own central nerve systems. Nor are they rich in academic and cultural stimuli. Because local economies are incomplete by themselves, whatever money they generate is mostly drained off by the big cities. Even when they affect the local economy, important business negotiations and financial arrangements are usually done at corporate headquarters located in large cities, with little benefit to the local economy. Such conditions in outlying areas further accelerate the concentration of economic, social, and cultural activities in big cities. In this vicious cycle, large cities already too crowded to function effectively gain new functions while local cities lose even their minimum essential functions.

In order to build a well-balanced nation, it is necessary to review the concentration of too many functions in big cities and to decentralize them so that different regions of the country may become more autonomous and internally self-sufficient. In so doing, we must see to it that the functions are coordinated and shared between big cities and local cities, as well as among local cities and their surrounding towns and villages.

The function of the modern city has changed with the passage of time. In an earlier stage of capitalism, cities were the centers of productive activity. Cities grew as more plants and factories were built in and around them. Later, other factors began to weigh more heavily. Distribution and consumption became major functions. Today, the city is the nerve center more than anything else. The importance of the city as a nerve center has been dramatically increased with the advent of the information age.

Furthermore, international economic activities are imposing an increasingly important role upon large cities by making them the central marketplaces of international activities and information. As the result of its rapid economic growth, Japan is no longer obscurely located in the "Far East" but will inevitably be called upon to play the role of a nerve center in international politics, economics, and finance.

If Tokyo, Osaka, and other urban concentrations are to become viable marketplaces in this age of information and internationalization, they must eliminate and simplify their overcomplicated functions. This should be done by relocating those industrial plants, universities, and research institutes which no longer need to be located in large cities. Many of the regulatory powers should also be delegated to local governments to streamline their administration.

Linking the Nation With Computers

Well-planned improvement and expansion of the information network throughout Japan is prerequisite to all efforts to reduce the imbalance between big cities and outlying areas. As an immediate target, telephones must be installed upon request anytime and anywhere. Nation-wide direct dialing should also be made possible between any two points. At the same time, cable television, picture-phones, data communication (linking homes and offices with computers), and other features of the information age should be extensively introduced. A vigorous effort is needed to develop information systems and to utilize new communication techniques so that each locality is better equipped with the necessary tools of the information age.

One practical solution to our immediate problem is a rationalization of communication costs. At present, about 2.5 million telephones are installed in the twenty-three wards of Tokyo with its total area of 225 square miles. It costs only three cents to make calls within this area, no matter how long one talks. But in some areas of the country, the number of phones a person can call for only three cents is as low as 1,000. The obvious conclusion is that the cost of exchanging information is much lower in Tokyo.

Furthermore, under current rates, long distance calls are disproportionately costly. For example, it costs $10.80 for the first three minutes of a call to call New York City from Tokyo over a distance of 9,400 miles. But between Tokyo and Kyoto, separated by only 250 miles, the same three-minute call costs $1.06. Yet two points in Tokyo 15 miles away from each other, for example, Ogikubo and Koiwa, can be connected by a regular call for only three cents. While it would admittedly be very difficult to adopt immediately a uniform criterion for fare schedules throughout the country, long distance rates must be reduced at least enough so that people can call any part of the country without worrying as much as they do now about cost. This would help close the information gap between the center and the fringes.

If Japan is reorganized into what might be called an "information archipelago" based upon the three pillars of an improved information network, positive development of new communication devices and information systems, and the rationalization of communication costs, people in remote areas will no longer have to travel to Tokyo to obtain information for business or study.

Computerized data processing will play the leading role in the information age. Just as super-express trains carry people over rails at tremendous speeds, communication circuits connecting computers with homes and offices will carry both input and output information.

Prototypes of such data communication are already being put to practical use. The JNR and the Japan Air Lines use such systems for passenger reservations. Banks use them for exchange and deposit operations. A push-button dial system that can connect subscribers' telephones with computers for business calculation has already been developed and put into service in Tokyo and Osaka.

Cable television and picture-phones will also play a major role in the information age. Although further technological development and cost reductions are necessary before picture-phones can be widely used, people are already excited about the possibility of talking, face to face, to people far away. This device will also be used as a forum for conferences whereby corporate headquarters, local offices, and plants can communicate with each other without actually bringing people together.

A new information system combining data communication and cable television will also become a reality. Currently, MITI is developing a video information system in which a television set not only receives both wireless and cable pictures but is connected to an information center or data bank that can give instant answers to such questions such as "What is the total area of Japan?" or "What is the International Monetary Fund?"

These new information networks and systems are important because they greatly facilitate the movement of industry and population from urban concentrations to local areas. A ready availability of information irrespective of location will make it possible to relocate not only manufacturing plants but also planning, research, and managerial departments of business firms. Once this is done, graduates of local universities may choose to seek employment in their own locality. Corporations need not necessarily establish their headquarters in big cities. Thanks to an information network connecting them with suppliers and wholesalers, companies can conduct business negotiations close to the points of production, with more efficient and profitable transactions resulting.

When information from the national government becomes easily available in any part of the country, be it Kyushu or Hokkaido, local and municipal governments can formulate more effective planning on the basis of a better understanding and awareness of what is going on in the rest of the country. More

Cheers! (*with Premier Chou En lai, 1973*)

To the end of past enmity
and the beginning of future friendship

Tanaka with President Nixon and Foreign Minister Ohira (*in Hawaii, 1972*)

With Soviet Ambassador Troyanovsky (*1973*)

Top: Tanaka and his daughter entertaining U.N. Secretary General and Mrs. Waldheim in Tokyo

Above: With U.K. Prime Minister Heath

Left: With U.S. Presidential Adviser Kissinger and U.S. Ambassador Ingersoll (*right*)

Appealing to the man
on the street ————
decision, then action!

Making his keynote address to the Diet
(*House Speaker Nakamura in the background*)

A sense of informality,
humor,
and compassion. . .

Top: On the links with golfer Jack
Nicklaus (*center*)

Left: Author and wife being amused
by their golfer grandson

Praying with his mother, Fume,
before the Buddhist altar in his
native home

Together with family: his wife Hana, daughter
Makiko, son-in-law Naoki, and grandson

Prime Minister Chou En-lai of China and
Prime Minister Kakuei Tanaka of Japan

A thousand hopes for world peace and eternal friendship!

photo: Konosuke Ishii
Tomihiro Kubota

responsive and creative local government will result. Scholars and researchers in local universities, who have long suffered from a pathetic shortage of information, will no longer have to labor under this handicap.

Probably the greatest benefits to the average man will be the use of information systems in education and medicine. Local areas will, for instance, be able to provide technical and language education of the same high standards as in large cities, although the individual teacher will remain indispensable for developing character.

The benefits in the field of medicine are even more obvious. When people get sick in underpopulated rural areas today, they have to travel several miles by bus to a hospital in a nearby town. Even then, these hospitals are not adequately equipped with modern medical facilities. Particularly in highly sophisticated areas such as heart surgery, Japan's total number of qualified doctors is limited. With the development of a medical information system, however, it will become possible to send a patient's data to a medical center located in the prefectural capital for diagnosis and prescription. It will not be long before doctors are sent by helicopter to remote areas like isolated islands to attend emergency cases.

If a cable television facility is installed for every community of 5,000 to 10,000 households, the station can carry information on various community activities, such as tennis clubs, folk-singing groups, and amateur baseball teams, so that more people can be invited to participate. Obviously, physical amenities such as playgrounds and concert halls should be improved, but sport and hobby clubs are just as important in building and strengthening local community solidarity.

It is only when information services are developed so that they are able to promote community culture and when this information is put to effective use by the local government and for the local economy that people will begin to develop a strong sense of attachment to their own communities and local development will begin making real progress.

Local Cities: New Frontiers

In the process of Japan's modernization over the last hundred years, the energy that has made Japan what it is today has always been supplied by the people who were born and brought up in rural areas and later moved to big cities. But the future of Japan over the next hundred years depends upon whether or not people born and brought up in urban areas will seek new frontiers in rural Japan and settle there to build a new Japan. This in turn depends upon whether or not industry will grow in outlying areas to create high income opportunities; whether or not local cities will develop adequate urban functions in cultural, economic, and social spheres; and whether or not the information gap between small local cities and big cities can be closed and living in rural Japan can be made as rich, convenient, and comfortable as living in urban Japan.

Three possibilities suggest themselves for strengthening and improving local cities. One is to strengthen the central functions of prefectural capitals, particularly such cities as Sapporo, Sendai, Hiroshima, and Fukuoka which are also regional cores. The second involves improving the living environment and urban functions of medium-sized cities so as to make them sub-centers of prefectural life—for example, Asahikawa and Kushiro in

Hokkaido, Hachinohe and Hirosaki in Aomori Prefecture. In both of these approaches, the purpose is to revitalize existing local cities with more adequate urban functions and a better living environment so that people may choose to stay and settle there rather than having to flow into Tokyo or Osaka as they do now. The third possibility is to create "quarter-million cities" having as their core industrial parks to be constructed through the process of industrial relocation. The creation of such new cities is the key to local development efforts in the years to come, along with urban redevelopment, which is one of the two most important components in the plan to remodel the Japanese archipelago.

Cities of 250,000

The new quarter-million cities are to be constructed as the strategic bases for local development. The mere movement of industrial facilities from urban concentrations to less intensely populated areas alone will not create such bases. In addition to the production activities of the relocated industry, a new city must develop sufficient urban functions to serve the local population, including information, finance, and distribution, and must be equipped with adequate medical, cultural, and educational facilities.

In other words, each new city is intended to be a center in its relation to the immediately surrounding area of independent economic activity as well as of materially and culturally rich life so that people will remain in the countryside and population concentration will be avoided.

There are two alternate ways to build such new cities of 250,000. One is to expand and strengthen existing smaller cities which have already accumulated a certain amount of urban

amenities. Take, for example, an area that has one or two existing cities with a total population of 70,000 to 100,000, such as the
Sakata-Tsuruoka area in Yamagata Prefecture. Such urban areas
may be extended outward to accommodate new residents, and
industrial parks may be constructed apart from commercial and
residential districts but functionally connected with the urban
section so that the entire area is organized as an integral whole
and population may be attracted. The second avenue is to consolidate a number of towns and villages, each with a population
of about 20,000, into a new urban center and to locate industrial
parks along the outer edge. An example is the area of Aira-
cho, Hayato-cho, and Kokubu-shi in Kagoshima Prefecture. The
ideal situation is when spacious sites are available and it is possible to construct the new community close to an expressway
interchange or with convenient automobile access to a railway
station on the new super-express train network.

Population size, of course, can be varied between 150,000 or
300,000, depending upon local conditions and other factors af-
fecting new-city formation. The figure of 250,000 is used merely
to suggest that new cities must keep their populations below a
certain optimum level beyond which overcrowding begins to
create pollution problems and destroy the sense of community.
The essential thing is to construct new cities where man, greenery, and industry can exist in harmony under the control of man.

The concept of quarter-million, therefore, represents an entirely new approach. Thus it is essential to formulate plans for
land use and urban development for each given area, with zoning
into residential, commercial, and industrial districts. Streets,
sewers, water supply systems, parks, and green belts should then
be constructed prior to other construction. The industrial district is to be patterned after an industrial park so that pollution-

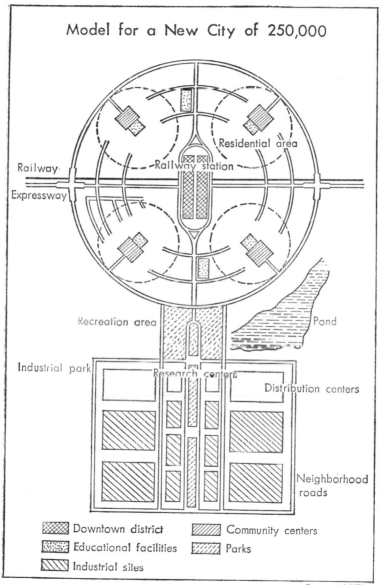

Model for a New City of 250,000

Residential area

Railway

Railway station

Expressway

Recreation area

Pond

Industrial park

Research centers

Distribution centers

Neighborhood roads

▨ Downtown district   ▨ Community centers
▨ Educational facilities   ▨ Parks
▨ Industrial sites

Source: MITI

prevention facilities, for example, can be incorporated into the early design phase of the park. For the residential district, the ratio of building to lot should be so fixed as to provide sufficient space between homes. Every effort must be made to make these new cities ideal communities. The new cities must develop those functions which the existing local cities lack.

First of all, they should have sufficient urban functions to make them focal points for local development. This means providing not only the city residents but also the neighboring rural population with adequate facilities and opportunities for information, consumption, medical treatment, education, culture, and leisure. To be more concrete, they must prepare the same mix of schools, general hospitals, concert halls, department stores, specialty shops, movie theaters, bowling alleys, and other facilities as large cities typically have.

Secondly, the economic activities should be large enough to be self-sustaining. Pollution-free industrial parks will become a core for such activities, supplemented by banks, department stores, and other functions that support a viable economy.

Thirdly, these cities, with the blessings of nature, must illuminate the culture of their own localities. Traveling through small local cities of Europe and America, we see people lying on the grass and soaking up the sun, enjoying art exhibits at museums and theater performances—all of the same high quality as in large cities. These areas often have their own distinctive arts, whether they be folk dances or dramas, of which their people are proud. I would like to see Japanese local cities enrich and develop their own distinct cultures. Houses, streets, sewers, and water systems alone are not equal to this task. Theaters, museums, and other facilities must be added.

Fourthly, they must be new communities where warm human

relations develop among the residents. It is true that housing projects and new towns that have been built to date have alleviated the housing shortage. But more often than not, relations among the residents are sterile. In extreme instances, there is no visiting in the neighborhood whatsoever, and people do not even know their neighbors' names. Obviously these people also have little sense of community. New cities of 250,000 should not be made into such human wastelands. They must be new communities where people can live and work with meaning and purpose in life, can share their joys and each other's company, and can talk over the problems of their own city and the future of their country. They must offer facilities for neighborly dialogue, including plazas and parks, and for cultural and sport activities. The installation of a cable television system would also greatly facilitate intra-city communication.

A Capital for Every Industry

The quarter-million cities may also develop into capitals of modern growth industries. An industrial capital is a city which houses the nation's largest concentration of productive facilities in any given industry. Industrial capitals are common in the other advanced nations. In the United States, Detroit is the industrial capital for the automobile industry, Pittsburgh for iron and steel, Hollywood for films, Boston and vicinity for electronics, and California for the aircraft industry. Most of these industrial capitals also have corporate headquarters, research and development, educational, financial, and commercial institutions as well as government agencies related to that particular industry. They also attract people. Corporate executives, engineers, and so on live in the neighborhood, creating a sense of community and contributing to activities for cultural improvement.

At present, Japan has no industrial capitals in the strict sense of the term. I would like to propose some concrete ideas for building these in the future. Suppose we plan to build an industrial capital for an interior-design industry. National and municipal institutions for research and development related to that industry, business centers, exhibition halls, and educational and training facilities for designers and skilled workers would all be located in the chosen city. All government agencies and branches related to the industry would move to this city to facilitate streamlining administative and regulatory activities.

One practical way to go about constructing such an industrial capital is to hold a major event like an international trade fair on interior design in the city which is scheduled to be made into the industrial capital. This would have many advantages. The name of the city would become better known and more closely associated with the industry, and various fair buildings could later be used as exhibition halls and training centers. Furthermore, such an industrial capital would be the natural place to hold regular trade fairs and art exhibitions to facilitate trade negotiations and international exchanges. Companies, designers, and technical people connected with the interior-design industry would move to the city, and it would steadily grow into an industrial capital for that industry in the true sense of the term.

Another example is the International Ocean Expo scheduled to be held in Okinawa in 1975 with the theme of "The Sea We Would Like to See." Among the major attractions of the Expo will be a multi-purpose thermal plant (for desalination of sea water, centralized heating and air-conditioning, etc.), a marine city with numerous leisure facilities, and a maritime research and training center. Using this marine fair as a trigger, I would like to see Okinawa developed as industrial capital for ocean development.

Nucleus Cities: Retaining the Old, Adapting the New

Local cities have grown as centers in their respective areas, and these local communities have clustered into blocs, each constituting a sphere of more or less self-contained life. Excepting major metropolitan areas, the Ministry of Construction divides the country into 164 such blocs. Each bloc has an average area of 770 square miles with a population of 400,000 people and includes eighteen cities, towns, and villages. Each bloc has one nucleus city, which is the seat of the prefectural government and the center of that bloc's activities. Improving the functions of these nuclear cities will be the key to regional development around existing cities.

Nuclear cities such as Sapporo, Sendai, Kanazawa, Hiroshima, Takamatsu, and Fukuoka must be made more effective nerve centers of their respective regions. For each region, these cities must become real centers in terms of universities, general hospitals, and other educational, cultural, medical, and leisure facilities.

It is often erroneously asserted that the information society is necessarily a centralized society. On the contrary, it is precisely because of improved information systems that the regulatory powers of the national government can and should be more decentralized and local governments can and should be given an even freer hand in planning on the basis of as much information as is available to the central government. In order to improve the position of these cities as the nerve centers of regional life, the kinds of industry to be invited should be information or service-oriented industries such as think-tanks, consulting organizations, research and development institutions, and computer centers.

Some of these nuclear cities are already beginning to be somewhat overcrowded. This calls for renewal of downtown areas, suburban improvement, and subway and monorail construction for intra-city transit. Similar phenomena are observed, and similar solutions should be applied, in such prefectural capitals as Aomori, Akita, Morioka, Yamagata, Fukushima, Niigata, Kofu, and Toyama.

Among other things, the focal cities must maintain their distinctive traditional cultures and help to foster a new culture characteristic of their respective areas. The traditional culture should be passed down and preserved not merely as a tourist attraction but more importantly as a symbol of local pride and a national treasure. For this, the Government should subsidize the conservation of local art forms and historic monuments, as well as the construction and renovation of folk art museums and libraries. In order to develop a new culture, theaters, concert halls, and various other facilities should be added. Modern shopping centers and amusement parks must be rapidly developed if these cities are to attract young people.

Public investment should be concentrated on improving urban infrastructure such as roads and sewage systems. At present, the per-capita investment in public works in the local cities is only one-third that of the metropolitan areas.

As far as the nuclear cities are concerned, improvement of their educational, medical, cultural, and leisure facilities is obviously in order if they are to serve the needs of the surrounding population effectively. They should also attempt to invite, in an orderly manner, knowledge-intensive industry by constructing industrial parks on their outskirts.

Inside each bloc, recreational facilities such as lakes, marinas, fishing and camping grounds, hiking trails, and ski resorts can be built. I would also like to locate some rehabilitation and recuperation facilities there.

Academic Towns in a Natural Setting

Relocation of universities is another effective means to alleviate the overconcentration of the big cities. Although each prefecture has at least one national university as the result of the postwar revision of the educational system, it is only those prestige schools in the metropolises that attract students and faculty. Local universities in fact are more or less standing still. At present, Japan has some 390 universities with a total enrollment of 1,700,000. Of these, Tokyo alone accounts for about one hundred universities and 630,000 students. The presence of so many schools and students is one of the most important factors in Tokyo's overcrowded situation.

We can disperse some of these universities to existing local cities with better environments and make them university cities, or to places with open space and sunshine and build new academic towns in the midst of nature.

In prewar Japan, prestigious high schools which prepared students for entry into Imperial Universities were located in medium-sized local cities such as Sendai, Kanazawa, Kumamoto, Okayama, and Kagoshima. With distinctive traditions and academic climates, these schools attracted young people and, as such, contributed greatly to the cultural enrichment of their host cities. The world-famous universities of Oxford and Cambridge are located in small cities only an hour or an hour and a half by train from London. They are in effect, cities in themselves. No matter how small the city in which it is located, the university whose substance is rich can live up to international standards.

The relocation of Tokyo-based universities to less populated areas is one way to relieve the overpopulation of this metropolis.

At the same time, I would like to see each one of the existing local universities become a leading institution of learning in a certain discipline, so that attending that university would become practically indispensable for any in-depth study in the given field. If this is done, the problem of too many students being concentrated in Tokyo's universities will be alleviated to some extent.

Another approach is to build new academic towns in spacious and beautiful natural surroundings near lakes or in the mountains. Adequate information and transportation networks should be provided so that the remote location is not a handicap in terms of availability of academic information. Dormitories, libraries, and athletic fields are essential for students to develop sound minds and bodies. Better housing and research facilities must be added for the faculty members so that they may choose to stay and engage in research activities. It is only when the academic environment is prepared in this way that the decentralization of universities will be possible.

Revitalization of Rural Life

The concentration of industry and population in megalopolises has drained the rural areas of their youth and energy for growth. One of the important concepts in remodeling the Japanese archipelago is to provide rural areas with the conditions necessary for revitalization so that they can share urban Japan's prosperity. Farms produce foods indispensable for national survival. They are also the source of income for farmers. Ideally, agriculture should be an occupation worthy of respect, both as a means of earning a living and as the source of the nation's food. We should maintain self-sufficiency of at least 80 percent of our major food items for a sound national economy.

More than any other industry, agriculture is dependent upon natural conditions. Even assuming that there will be no major wars, if Japan depends upon imports for the greater part of its food supply, there is always the danger that we might be caught short if harvests are poor in the exporting countries. On the other hand, when their harvests are good, a large flow of surplus food products might be shipped into Japan and disrupt our domestic agriculture. If food supply and demand, and consequently prices, were to fluctuate frequently, there would be no stability for our farmers or for our people as a whole.

We should also remember that agricultural production, once reduced, takes a long time and great effort to restore to former levels. Agriculture is not the kind of industry in which one can expect an immediate return on investment.

Postwar Japanese economic history shows that it was not until the nation had graduated from the period of acute food shortage and achieved self-sufficiency that the economy as a whole began to record rapid growth. It may well be that many nations today suffer from food shortages. In many cases, they have neglected agricultural efforts in their haste to industrialize, and the resultant failure in agriculture has, in turn, put a damper on industrial growth. Some people criticize Japanese postwar agricultural policy as being overprotective of agricultural interests. But it should be remembered that our present prosperity is in large part due to the fact that farmers did their best to continue to supply rice during the difficult period immediately after the War. In this sense it can be argued that agricultural policy has not been in conflict with the interests of urban residents.

Nor should it be forgotten that agricultural use of land means a great deal in terms of conserving nature, preventing natural disasters, and maintaining a better living environment for all the people. Wide paddy fields throughout the country are huge reservoirs that keep the climate mild and prevent floods. Vegetables growing in the fields are an important source of oxygen as well as of pastoral comfort. Rural areas have always been the spiritual home for the people who moved to the big cities during the rapid urban growth of the last century. As we look ahead to the next one hundred years, we must remember how important a role rural Japan has played in the past and renew our determination to make our farmlands a viable source of life for the Japanese people.

A Comprehensive Agricultural Policy

It goes without saying that Japan's agriculture is now facing a historic turning point. Production of rice, the staple food of our people, has been conspicuously in excess of demand, and crop reductions have had to be enforced since 1968. As Japan became increasingly involved in the international economy, foreign pressures have mounted for liberalization of agricultural imports. To meet such demands, Japanese agriculture must improve its productivity and make itself competitive with foreign agriculture.

In terms of domestic economic policy as well, farm income must be raised to a level equal to that of secondary and tertiary industries, commensurate with the pace of economic growth. Otherwise, few people can be expected to choose the farmer's life, and rural communities, as the basis of our food supply, will collapse for these reasons. Therefore, we must design and implement a comprehensive agricultural policy as soon as possible.

The United States is the leading nation in urging Japan to accelerate the liberalization of agricultural imports. The U.S. balance of trade has deteriorated sharply because of reduced industrial competitiveness and this, together with the outflow of dollars for overseas investment, has weakened the position of the dollar. This weakness led to the multilateral currency realignment in December, 1971. On the other hand, American agricultural products have a very strong competitive position and account for a significant portion of U.S. exports. By comparison, Japanese agricultural products are relatively more expensive. Even rice, which is produced more efficiently than other crops, costs two or three times as much as in the United States. According to one study, it is estimated that rice production in Japan takes 530 hours of labor for a yield of 3,850 pounds per acre, or a productivity of 7.3 pounds per man-hour. This is one-thirtieth of American productivity, which is 16 hours of labor for a yield of 3,520 pounds per acre, or 220 pounds per man-hour,

If this is the case with rice, how could Japan possibly compete with the United States in wheat, soybeans, and rapeseeds? It is still well remembered that the liberalization of imports of products such as oranges and beef were the focus of the recent Japan-U.S. trade negotiations. It seems inevitable under the circumstances that imports of agricultural products will have to be gradually liberalized by expanding quotas.

The 1971 Agricultural White Paper puts the average gross annual income of Japanese agricultural households at $5,350. Of this, the actual agricultural income was only $1,690. The remaining $3,660, or 56.3 percent, came from non-agricultural sources, including, among other things, seasonal employment away from home, which means that more than half of a farm household's income came from non-agricultural labor. On a national average, daily agricultural income was only 61 percent of the daily wage in manufacturing industries (average for manufacturing firms with five or more regular employees). This ratio was improved to 87 percent in fiscal 1972, but the disparity between industrial and agricultural productivity has begun to widen since then and the income gap has consequently become more pronounced.

It is estimated that the growing Japanese economy will give Japan a per-capita national income by 1985 greater than that of the United States today. Will the farmers enjoy their fair share of this growth? What should be done to increase farm income? These are questions our agricultural policy must answer.

For Economy of Scale

Given the limited availability of land in Japan, agricultural productivity and income can be increased only by an expansion of farm size and mechanization in order to produce more with less labor. This will inevitably mean a sharp decrease in the agricultural population. The 1971 farm labor force of 7,680,000 was 15.9 percent of the total labor force. Some scholars have even predicted that by 1985 the agricultural work force will be reduced to one-tenth of what it is today. About two-thirds of all farm workers today are women and old men; there are very few young people. The number of high-school graduates who go on to farm work has steadily declined from 48,000 in 1968 to 42,000 in 1969, to 37,000 in 1970, and to only 32,000 in 1971. From the first year of Meiji (1868) until 1952, some 400,000 young men and women joined the agricultural work force every year, to man the five to six million family farms. Today, this number is down to less than ten percent of its former average.

A family farm worker's hourly income is estimated at 67 cents to $1.33. If he works 2,000 hours a year, as is standard in other industries, he would earn an annual income of $1,340 to $2,660. When non-agricultural jobs promising annual incomes of $3,300 become readily available for farm wives, farms run primarily by wives with their husbands otherwise employed will rapidly disappear.

The United States, which is more than self-sufficient in food-stuffs and exports huge surpluses, has only 3.5 percent of its total labor force on the farm. As the Japanese industrial structure becomes more sophisticated and per-capita national income surpasses current American levels, the number of farmers as a percentage of the total work force will naturally decline to approximately U.S. levels.

If our agriculture is to continue to provide a stable food supply despite the declining farm population, there is no alternative but to make agriculture more capital-intensive and productive through mechanization and expansion. Two policies are neces-sary for this: one to absorb surplus labor leaving the farm and the other to mechanize and expand operations.

With respect to the first, the most desirable approach is to absorb such surplus labor locally, as suggested earlier in relation to the industrial relocation plan. With the relocation of manu-facturing plants to rural areas, local cities can be developed, and new tertiary industries will grow up alongside primary indus-tries. As plants are built in rural communities, whether as industrial parks or individually, those leaving agriculture can readily find employment. Having industry close to farms will also contribute to higher agricultural productivity and modernization.

What should future patterns of farm management be? With increased income and higher living standards, the dietary habits of the people will change rapidly, creating a strong demand for better quality and greater diversity. Consumption of cereals will decline, to be replaced by a greater intake of meat, eggs, milk, butter, fruit, and Western vegetables like tomatoes and lettuce.

Per-capita consumption of cereals in Sweden and Canada is less than half that in Japan, and still lower in the United States. This trend suggests that we should be selective in expanding production, emphasizing particularly livestock and fruit. The shift of orientation from rice to livestock is an unavoidable demand of the times. To meet this demand, it will be necessary to develop our mountain areas to create extensive pasture lands. When a stable supply of meat and dairy products is secured and imports of feed grains are reduced, the way will be open for high-productivity, high-income agriculture.

As of 1971, the total area under cultivation was 14,178,000 acres. Even assuming that this area will be somewhat reduced, the land available for each farmer should increase dramatically as a considerable portion of the farming population moves to other sectors and land is used more efficiently through the introduction of advanced stock-raising and greenhouse techniques.

However, given the pattern of scattered and small land ownership, as well as the prohibitively high land prices, expansion of farm size could be very difficult if left to itself. Tomorrow's capital-intensive agriculture must, of necessity, involve cooperatives, sub-contractors, salaried cultivators, and extensive land-leasing.

A comprehensive land use plan, on both national and prefectural levels, is prerequisite for agricultural development. Such a plan should determine which farmland should be converted to various other uses, including roads, residential areas, industrial zones, and greenery. With a total mobilization of scientific and technical know-how, the plan should define these various districts in order to make the most effective use of highway, railway, and air network connections. Once blueprints are drawn, the government should proceed with the acquisition of the necessary land. The farmland that remains can be earmarked as "permanent farm lands," and the government can subsidize both intensive and extensive infrastructural improvement of such agricultural land.

Vigorous investment in plant and equipment coupled with constant technological innovation has dramatically strengthened the international competitiveness of Japanese secondary industries such as iron and steel, shipbuilding, and synthetic fibers. There is no reason that what has been done in manufacturing cannot be done in agriculture. This time, the target is the improvement of agricultural infrastructure, for this is the key to the creation of high-productivity, high-efficiency agriculture.

Infrastructural improvement should include dry fields as well as paddies, so that rice may be rotated with other crops on flat areas. Each lot should be 2.5 to 7.5 acres for a more efficient utilization of large farm equipment; irrigation made efficient by the use of pipes and sprinklers controlled by computers that program timing and amount of irrigation; and drainage systems installed 3.5 feet or more below ground so that land can be more easily dried or flooded for more efficient crop rotation.

To achieve the twin goals of mechanization and expansion in agricultural operations, the existing policies and regulations need to be reviewed, including the possible abolition of the Agricultural Land Law, although the vested interests and rights of farmers must be respected here. Certain legislative actions may also be needed to offset the ill effects of abolishing the Agricultural Land Law in order to conserve good farmland and to keep farmland which has been improved with Government subsidies from being converted to other uses.

The high-productivity agriculture thus achieved will result in large cost and price reductions and become internationally competitive. Farmers will enjoy the same high income levels enjoyed by workers in secondary and tertiary industries.This will mean that both those remaining on the farms and those leaving the farms will share in the rich and comfortable life of tomorrow.

Reshaping Hamlets: Computerized Agriculture

In an age when computerized agriculture becomes a reality, the pattern of rural life and its centuries-old traditions will inevitably undergo a profound transformation.

Traditionally, it has not been rare for people to be born, to work, and to die in the same village. Today, members of more and more farm families commute to nearby towns and cities to work. Many husbands leave their farms for half-year or even year-long employment in large metropolitan areas. Television brings the urban life-style into rural hamlets with the flip of a switch, and the thought and behavior patterns of rural life are becoming less and less traditional and more and more urban. Many young men leave the farm and many young women choose not to marry into farm families, not merely because of economic reasons or working conditions but because they see urban life as more convenient, glamorous, and chic in every way.

We must provide them the same cultural sophistication as the big cities. In order to encourage young people to stay on the farms, to marry and to raise children there, and to contribute to the prosperity of their villages, we must build the foundations for a rich, human environment in these communities to help them to creater their own culture.

Just as urban planning is needed for cities, rural planning must be developed taking the local situation into account and reflecting the desires of the local people. Let me try here to give a brief description of life in the ideal agricultural village as I see it.

Both farm and lot size are expanded. The newest machinery is installed in fruit-sorting plants, rice mills, and flour mills. Receiving, packaging, and loading are all automated, and trucks carry products fresh from the fields. Food processing and freezing plants are also located in the village, as are machinery repair stations. The shopping center is conveniently situated. The neat rows of houses are clean and furnished with running water, flush toilets, and a sewage system. If you get sick, you do not have to ride the bus for an hour to see a doctor in town, for there is a clinic or hospital nearby. Day nurseries are available for the children of working women. As you walk by the cultural center, you can hear senior citizens teaching the traditional art forms of the village to the young people, for the village festival is approaching. In a gymnasium nearby, housewives and other young people are playing volleyball. Some of these young people work in the industrial park only a few miles away from the village.

You can also see people commuting to the farm from the nearby city. Ample highways connecting village and city make commuting easy. Now the rural village is an integral part of the greater local city area, closely linked with transportation and communication systems. Tokyo or Osaka is within one day's journey from the village. You can take pleasure trips wherever and whenever you like. Luxury or fashion items once available only in large cities quickly find their way to the village. The village, once deserted and forsaken, has been revitalized as a modern rural community co-existing and co-prospering in harmony with the larger urban areas.

With increased national income, a higher standard of living, and shorter working hours as firms adopt the five-day week, people will become more and more interested in how to spend their leisure time. Urbanites will feel very strongly about wanting to leave their towns of steel and cement on weekends to enjoy the sunshine and fresh air of the countryside, in order to enrich their lives and revitalize themselves for tomorrow.

Besides being a producer of foods and a living community, the rural village will become increasingly important as a place for people to rest and play. A comprehensive system providing for recreation within nature must be worked out for every rural district, integrating the villages with nearby mountains, woods, forests, lakes, and seashores. There is a movement to develop "recreational agriculture," in the sense of making it into a tertiary industry. For example, an agricultural park could be built in a village for city people to visit on weekends as do-it-yourself farmers. Meadows, fishing ponds, golf courses, and other natural recreational facilities can also be situated next to such a park. This will not only provide farmers with additional sources of income but will also give city dwellers the opportunity to return to nature and revitalize themselves. It will also contribute to harmony between city and village people. However, every care must be taken to avoid the wanton and unnecessary destruction of nature and the creation of cheap and gaudy eyesores.

From Horizontal to Vertical Cities

Repairing an old house is one of the most difficult things to do. It is much easier and cheaper to build an entirely new house than to overhaul an old house someone is living in. When it comes to the question of a metropolis with hundreds of years of history behind it, the difficulties are much greater. According to one expert estimate, the total remodeling of Tokyo would cost twenty times as much as building a new city from scratch. The problem is further complicated when the city in question is in the process of rapid growth and expansion.

Birmingham, England, located between London and Liverpool, was once a lively city as a major coal mining center. As coal lost its place as the primary source of energy, so did Birmingham. Although the British government planned its redevelopment as a city of 1,200,000 people, this did not get far. It was only when the city was actually on the brink of becoming a ghosttown that the government succeeded in acquiring 70 percent of the land necessary for the plan. A full-fledged effort was begun, and the city is in the midst of redevelopment.

The Soviet Union had planned to limit the population of Moscow, its capital city, to five million. But after World War II, it increased to over six million and began to cause serious problems of overcrowding. The Soviet government then planned to construct eight satellite cities in the Moscow suburbs to be modeled after the "new town" projects of London. Things did not go as planned, however, and the government was finally forced in 1960 to acquiesce to the expansion of Moscow's population and area. These two episodes indicate the difficulties involved in reshaping existing cities, be it in England, which incorporates a high degree of social planning within its free-market framework, or in the Soviet Union, which nationalizes land and all other means of production within its socialist structure.

Brazil implemented a bold and ingenious plan to build Brasilia, a city of "sun, green, and tranquility," and to move its capital from Rio de Janeiro. This was similar to building a new house and moving into it rather than repairing the old one. It will take some time for the project's full benefits to be felt, but such an undertaking is nonetheless practical for a country such as Brazil where the social and economic climate is relaxed, making it possible to wait decades for Brasilia to grow into the planned city of 500,000. Things are very different in Japan, where metropolitan areas are growing at a pace that could each year absorb the population of a new Brasilia.

The effective reconstruction of cities will not be possible unless a situation is created elsewhere which reduces the inflow of people. If we resort to patchwork measures in our haste to solve the immediate problems of overcrowding, we shall never be able to break the vicious cycle of redevelopment and reconcentration. The more money spent for urban redevelopment, the greater the gap between metropolitan and outlying areas, and the more people will be drawn to the improved urban life environment. In effect, nothing will be gained except greater pollution, traffic congestion, housing problems, and water shortages. This vicious cycle will not stop until and unless local areas attract both industry and people so that each region of the country may develop a degree of economic self-sufficiency. It is in this context that the remaking of the big cities should be regarded as synonymous with local development.

Space and Efficiency

In reshaping the cities, top priority should be given to creating a safe and comfortable living environment for residents. The minimum requirement is to provide for their physical security. To minimize disasters, buildings should be made fire-and earthquake-proof and open spaces must be maintained for emergency evacuations. Streets should be widened and separate pedestrian walkways provided to reduce traffic accidents. In order to provide a more healthful life environment, pollution should be eliminated, small houses replaced, slums cleared, and water and sewer systems and garbage disposal facilities improved. Parks and green spaces for relaxation also serve to strengthen the cities' ability to withstand disasters. Redevelopment must also plan for an increased number of nurseries, playgrounds, libraries, museums, and sport and recreation centers.

Another important aspect of remaking the cities is to check the ever-increasing cost of living. The cities should not only be safe and pleasant but also highly efficient in terms of lower socio-economic costs. It is, of course, desirable to live near one's place of work in order to reduce losses of time, money, and energy.

We need open space, whether for widening streets or building parks, green belts, or residential areas. Tokyo and Osaka would have to make their streets three times as wide as they are to match New York in terms of the ratio of street space to total city area. Likewise, they would have to increase their parks more than ten-fold to meet New York's standards. The cities should also be compact to improve business efficiency and lower socio-economic costs. These are some of the basic requirements in remodeling the cities. If they are to be met simultaneously, cities must revamp their essentially horizontal expansion of today for a more vertical structure.

One of the greatest advantages of making the cities compact is that various urban facilities which incorporate the latest technology, such as area-wide central heating and air-conditioning, can be introduced and installed more efficiently. With longer ducts and longer transmission distances, air-conditioning is more costly not only because of the longer ducts involved but also because of the greater thermal loss. Shorter distances are also important because they reduce sharply the costs of installing such devices as airchutes for mail and newspaper delivery, cable television, picture-phones, water supply, and sewerage and waste disposal systems. These devices reduce urban costs and make the city a pleasant place to live in.

How do we go about "verticalizing" our cities? Obviously, major sections of the city can be redeveloped by constructing high-rise buildings. But at the same time, suburbs should be improved in order to prevent disorderly sprawl.

An Urban Renewal Corporation

In more concrete terms, the following suggestions could be implemented in cities like Tokyo and Osaka.

First, land utilization plans should zone the city's districts by use and spell out the proper ratios of construction, streets, and open spaces. There could also be restrictions on low buildings below a minimum ratio of cubic content to land area. Once this is done, old buildings may be cleared for replacement by new buildings of a certain minimum height, beginning with those sections designated as redevelopment areas. The whole operation should be completed within, say, ten or fifteen years.

Placing restrictions on low buildings is an entirely new approach to urban development. We have maximum speed limits for city streets and minimum speed limits for expressways. By the same token, we must restrict the minimum height of buildings. At present, the Building Standards Law prohibits, in principle, buildings higher than 102 feet. This Law, however, should be revised to ban buildings less than 66 feet (seven stories) from certain designated districts.

Higher buildings would provide the same capacity with more open space. Therefore, by utilizing vertical space, the cities can have more space for various public uses. The construction of tall buildings should be encouraged on a block-by-block and not on the individual building basis. Otherwise we are likely to end up with tall buildings on small lots, like so many candles, which would have little space available for underground parking, an essential feature of new buildings. At times, block-by-block re-building may not be possible. Even then minimum sizes for building lots should be fixed and enforced.

Regulating building heights, fixing building-lot ratios, and set-ting minimum building lot sizes will not be sufficient for the remodeling of the cities. The cooperation and participation of the private sector is essential. No matter how much national and local governments may spend, they still can not purchase all the space necessary for redeveloping Tokyo or Osaka. The actual rebuilding must be left to private initiative. What the government can do, however, is to channel effectively private energy into redevelopment efforts by mobilizing its total fiscal, monetary, and tax resources. To accomplish this, I suggest establishing an Urban Renewal Corporation. The Japan Housing Corporation and the Housing Loan Corporation are also expected to become active participants in the total effort.

Government incentives may include, for example, low-interest, long-term loans for reconstruction to raise building heights. This, of course, does not mean the owner of the building may not use his own funds or loans available from private financial insti-tutions. When a high-rise building uses its upper stories (fourth floor and above) for residential purposes, a reduction or exemp-tion from the property tax for that portion of the building may be provided for the life of the structure. Such tax policy takes into account the fact that the costs of construction become greater for each additional floor, and that the use of added floors for residential purposes will help solve the housing shortage. Public housing may be made available for those who have to vacate a building during reconstruction. After construction is completed, they may continue to stay in this public housing or may move back into new apartments in the new building. The logic here is clear. Very simply, we say, "We shall lend you money for rebuilding your block into a high-rise construction, your property tax will be reduced or eliminated, and we will offer you an alternative place to live if desired, but you must complete construction within a certain period of time." If the work is not completed by the date set, the Urban Renewal Corporation may finish the work. These are the arrangements which will make redevelopment of big cities possible.

Arresting Suburban Sprawl

Another important aspect of urban policy is to arrest disorderly suburban sprawl. Typically, European and American cities have clear and distinct boundaries. As you drive out of these cities, houses suddenly become sparse and you find yourself driving through a green countryside. When you drive out of Tokyo or Osaka, you see an unbroken expanse of low, flat buildings extending for 15 or 20 miles.

It is the practice of many European countries to clearly demarcate districts for various purposes under their land-use plans. Power and gas companies often do not provide service to areas far from the city because it does not pay. Without heating facilities, winter life in Europe can be unbearable. All of these factors combine to prevent ugly sprawl in Europe.

By sharp contrast, the growth of Japan's cities has been without direction or planning. Land prices have been the dominant factor. Power and gas companies are legally bound to provide service even to solitary homes far from town. In due time, such isolated dwellings will have ten, then twenty and more neighbors, and roads, bridges, and sewers will have to be built. Forests and farm lands, which are readily convertible to housing lots, are considered potential residential areas by many Japanese. Thus clusters of houses extend into outlying areas with access to railway stations and where land prices are more or less within reach. Consequently, homes get farther and farther away from places of work, business efficiency is reduced, and the socioeconomic costs of the cities go up. And it is the institution of the commuter's pass—providing railway fare discounts on a scale unheard of elsewhere—that supports the ever-growing separation of home and work.

Disorderly metropolitan sprawl can be controlled only when new residential districts are systematically developed with the emphasis on high-rise apartment buildings. When a given area is designated as a new residential district with a clearly defined land-use plan, it is necessary first to determine the ratio of street and open space to the total area, and to construct basic infrastructure facilities such as water and sewage systems prior to the construction of houses. When this is a private development, construction permits should be issued only after such facilities are provided under specified standards.

When a land owner sells or uses his land for housing purposes, strict zoning regulations should be imposed. Private developers must be required to obtain development licenses. Illegal construction must be penalized by prohibitions on electricity, gas, water, and telephone installation.

Life in Vertical Cities

What does a vertical city look like? Let us see how a shopping district changes shape. As it stands today, rows of two-story buildings with shops on the street level and residences above them stand on both sides of the main street. Behind them are cramped rows of one- and two-story, old stucco houses. When this district is verticalized, much space will become available for green belts, plazas, and wider streets, as well as for playgrounds where children can play without worrying about automobile traffic. The whole area is made sunnier and people are freed of the sense of being cramped. There may even be room for new shops and offices to move in, and business may improve.

When the 1.7-story building average is raised to seventeen stories, the result will be nine times as much open space. Under the industrial redistribution plan, the 80 square miles of industrial sites now existing in the built-up areas of the National Capital Sphere and Kinki region will be halved by 1985. Hibiya Park in Tokyo is about 40 acres. Implementing industrial redistribution and constructing high-rise buildings, Tokyo and Osaka can build many parks the size of Hibiya Park throughout their cities.

Parks, small and large, might have flower beds and fountains. Shady promenades and attractive shopping arcades might be their main features. Libraries, museums, art galleries, and handicraft and art workshops might surround the parks. Seminars, conferences, and meetings on diverse subjects such as art, education, technology, and medicine might be held each day, with people coming from all over the country and all over the world to attend. Lying on the grass or sitting on a shady bench, city dwellers may restore their sense of well-being and belonging. An asphalt jungle which decayed the minds and hearts of its inhabitants is now transformed into a lively forum where minds may meet. Office districts, shopping centers, parks, and residential areas are connected by subway and monorail networks. The CVS (computer-controlled vehicle system) also serves the city's transit needs. Push a button and ride a CVS; it will watch for your stop while you read your book. This is the kind of metropolitan life I want to see realized.

Construction of high-rise buildings *per se* is not the primary purpose of "verticalizing" the big cities. Rather, the most important aspect is to use the newly available open space for public welfare. Both aboveground and underground, precious metropolitan space must be fully utilized.

We will soon need a huge network of underground passages and multi-purpose tunnels. The earliest undertaking of this kind was the underground sewers of Paris constructed during Napoleon's reign. In Japan, verticalization of big cities is inconceivable without multi-functional, multi-purpose, underground tunnels.

Not only telephone lines, power transmission lines, gas, water, and sewage pipes, but central heating and air-conditioning ducts as well as cable-television lines can be installed in these multipurpose underground tunnels. Garbage can be collected by chutes which connect to these tunnels to facilitate the collection and disposal of our ever-increasing garbage and waste. It is not inconceivable that mail and newspapers could be delivered from the underground passage through air-chutes. Once such tunnels are built, it will no longer be necessary for the utility companies to be constantly tearing up the streets. This will reduce public spending. The disappearance of telephone poles and wires alone will make the streets wider and less cluttered.

Verticalization of cities requires that streets be proportionately wider. The current regulation is that a building may not be constructed within two yards of the center of the street. These must be revised to four yards for the narrowest street, so that there will be at least eight yards between buildings across a street. Buildings located at intersections should be set far enough back from the road to give drivers and pedestrians a clear field of vision and to ease traffic congestion.

Chicago provides a good example of how to build roads in a large city. In Chicago, one highway runs right through a post-office building. There is only one similar case in Japan, the Asahi Shinbun building in Osaka, with an expressway running through it. This innovation was the result of patient persuasion of the Asahi Shinbun management by the Hanshin Road Corporation. This kind of approach should be more widely accepted in the future. There are already a number of terminal and station buildings for railways, and if it is possible to have railways run through buildings, the same feasibility should exist for highways. But we must plan carefully because, while wooden structures may easily be torn down, high-rise buildings are more durable.

One problem we must face in remodeling the cities, of course, is that of traffic congestion. The basic approach should be to systematize urban transportation networks for different specific purposes. The Japanese National Railways, private lines, and subways should be primarily responsible for providing mass transportation for commuters. Within downtown areas, subway lines capable of transporting fifty to sixty thousand people each way every hour should play the major role. The idea is to integrate the different systems so that trains can ride on each others' tracks and to build a system of radial high-speed mass transit so that residential areas and urban centers and subcenters may be directly connected. This requires the building of an intensive subway network in downtown areas. If we were to transport fifty thousand people one way every hour by automobile, the Ministry of Transport estimates that streets would have to be made 660 feet wide—an impossible proposition.

The advantages of the monorail will be maximized when used in the loop system where the commuter density is lower than for the radial system. Monorail construction is also being seriously considered as a possible alternative to buses in local focal cities such as Sendai, Shizuoka, and Kita-Kyushu.

CVS has the dual advantages of being similar to private automobiles in being able to take people to their destinations and of running under control on exclusive tracks like railways. When it is installed to connect public housing, shopping centers, schools, and railway stations, it will be welcomed by the people as their "autotaxi." I would like to see CVS developed as a promising mode of transportation in the future.

Good Housing for All

The first objective of any housing policy is to provide every hard-working citizen with the opportunity to have a comfortable place to live.

More specifically, housing policy must be in harmony with the people's 'life cycle' and the different style of living each phase of this cycle typically represents. For example, young people often like to live in apartments separate from their parents, for they are in the prime of life and prefer greater mobility. In their forties and fifties, these same people, now more affluent than before, will choose to build their own homes in the suburbs, possibly with a small garden, where they may take care of their aged parents.

Where land prices are as high as they are in Japan, it is impossible to divorce housing policy from land policy. People with modest savings lament not being able to build their own homes, but it is not the house which is beyond their means. It is the lot on which to build which is the problem.

In densely populated and highly industrialized metropolitan areas, demand is concentrated on a limited amount of land, creating a great imbalance of supply and demand. If left to the workings of the free market, land prices will only rise, transforming land from a factor of human living and production into an object of speculation. So landowners tend to hang on to their land. Many of the same landowners who refuse to make their land available for public and social purposes often make fortunes by disposing of it when the price is high enough. For the ordinary citizen, the possibility of building his own house is becoming more and more remote. The number of new houses built in Tokyo, Osaka, and Nagoya in 1971 was 40,000 less than in the previous year. While recession can explain part of this drop, the primary culprit was the prohibitively sharp rise in land prices.

Land: Private Rights vs. Public Welfare

Land is not the kind of commodity that can be produced or transferred. Because of its inherently limited supply, land must be utilized effectively so as to contribute to the welfare and prosperity of the entire nation. Therefore, the priority should be given to public welfare rather than to private rights. Obviously, land ownership must be respected as part of the freedom to possess private property, but when private use of land comes into conflict with public use, obviously the latter should be given priority.

In order to use land effectively and to prevent land prices from soaring, the Comprehensive National Land Development Act must be revised to make possible land use on a national scale. At the same time, it is important to disperse industries and population that have been concentrated in cities so that the problem of depopulation may be solved and the balance may be restored between supply and demand for land.

This plan should not stop at mere division of land by end uses. It must be backed by enforcement. Under this plan, every part of Japan should be treated as an organic and systematic part of the whole. The national government designates conservation areas throughout the nation, such as farm lands and forests, while local governments provide detailed zoning regulations for industrial, commercial, residential, and other areas. The national and local governments should also provide guidance for effective land-use patterns such as the development of three-dimensional utilization of land for residential and transportation facilities and the prevention of sprawl and breaking up of land into overly small fragments.

As industry and population relocate to outlying areas and the number of dwellings is increased through urban verticalization, land prices in metropolitan areas will be stabilized. Those who leave the cities can acquire rural land at lower prices and will build far from the metropolitan areas. In seeking to solve land problems, such synergistic effects should be utilized to their fullest.

Another possibility worth examining for the national and local governments is purchasing land for constructing extensive public housing to be made available at low prices.

The City of Stockholm, Sweden, began purchasing land in 1904, and today has title to 200 square miles of land within and beyond the city limits. This is an area two and a half times the size of the city itself.

Italy has a law called the "Law to Accelerate Acquisition of Land for the Construction of Low-Rent Housing for Workers" (1962). Under this law, every municipality of 50,000 people or more must formulate a land use plan including low-rent housing, parks, and other social service facilities. The disposition of land covered by the plan is frozen for ten years. The municipal government can acquire up to half of this land by right of eminent domain. The other half can be acquired, as the need arises, by national, regional, or provincial governments, as well as by the Workers' Housing Association. It is said that land purchase price is set at the average of the official assessment of its market value and the ten-year aggregate rent, which usually falls somewhere between 50 to 70 percent of current market value.

West Germany and England provide two approaches to housing policy. Despite wartime destruction, West Germany had solved its quantitative housing problem by the early 1960's and is now in the process of qualitative improvement. The West German housing policy was to provide the private sector with a series of very generous fiscal, monetary, and tax incentives while leaving the initiative in private hands. In addition to income tax deductions for savings deposited for housing purposes, interest-free housing loans are provided by the individual *Land* governments. These were extremely long-term loans, requiring repayment of principal at the rate of only one percent a year. If the borrower makes an early repayment, half of the principal can be canceled and need not be repaid. Under such a housing policy where the private sector takes the initiative, the Government rarely needs to build public housing. And it is said that public housing today accounts for only 2 percent of West Germany's total number of dwellings.

By contrast, the public sector has been the prime mover in England's housing development. Of the total of 7,442,000 houses built between 1945 and 1970, 57 percent were public projects and 43 percent private.

The system of subsidized rent for the poor is a particularly noteworthy facet of the British housing policy. Setting rent standards for both private and public apartments, the government subsidizes poor people depending upon family size and income. For instance, if a family of five lives in an apartment with a standard weekly rent of $13 and if the family's weekly income is $44, then this family pays only two dollars in rent. If their weekly income is below $33 they need not pay any rent. The balance is paid by the government to the apartment owner, be it local government or private persons.

These foreign examples suggest new and innovative ways of developing and implementing land and housing policies suited to our own conditions.

National and local efforts to improve the infrastructure will require huge land areas. There are fiscal limitations to the government's ability to acquire land through cash compensation, and, in any case, massive expenditures by the government for land would be inflationary.

One way to cope with this problem is to go beyond the current practice of settling land acquisitions each year in the current account and to examine the feasibility of compensating owners with government bonds which might be issued within the framework of a long-range fiscal plan. Care must be taken, however, to modify the mechanism of the bond market in order to establish the conditions under which such bonds could be sold. Various welfare and pension funds should also be studied as possible capital sources for local governments so that they may secure the necessary land for housing and other public uses.

Leased Land

National and local governments can also secure land through leasing arrangements, as opposed to buying, and this approach might well be more extensively utilized, depending upon local conditions.

Some private companies are already adopting this method. For example, Bridgestone Tire Company has rented 125 acres of land for the company's new plant in the City of Kuroiso on the Nasu plateau in Tochigi Prefecture. The lease is for sixty years, and at present the monthly rent is two cents per square yard. Under the terms of contract, the rent is subject to renegotiation every three years, taking into account property taxes and the official assessment of the property for inheritance tax purposes.

Seventy percent of the plant site had been farm land, with most of the rest forested and a very small portion housing lots. The Nasu area where the plant is located is land opened in the early years of the Meiji Era, and the owners have developed a strong attachment to this land which their fathers and grandfathers toiled to clear. It is this very attachment which gave rise to Bridgestone's rental arrangement. In April, 1970, the contract was formally signed by the company and twenty-eight landowners, with the mayor of the host city of Kuroiso serving as witness. The farmers did not have to forfeit the trust of their forefathers because they still have title to the land, and at the same time they can be sure of a regular income comparable to what they would have made had they continued to work on the farm (this was the criteria for determining the rent). The company, on its part, can use the land just the same as if it had bought it yet did not have to make the huge lump-sum payment which buying would entail.

New York also offers a good example. In the slum redevelopment program, the Housing Authority purchases the entire district and provides the dwellers with temporary housing. The slum is then cleared, and the land is improved and sold to private developers who build high-rise apartments to rent at very low rates. This is possible because the Authority sells the land to private developers at a low enough price, calculated on future rents, that they will find it still a paying proposition. The Authority's deficit is subsidized two-thirds by the federal government and one-third by the city government.

The New York experiment also suggests bold new approaches applicable in Japan where rising land prices have forced even public housing projects to charge such high rents that some have been left unoccupied.

One method would be for the government to lease its land to the Japan Housing Corporation. As a practical procedure, the Industrial Relocation and Coal Mining Area Development Corporation may make land which it has purchased as a result of industrial relocation available to the Housing Corporation while retaining title to it. Housing Corporation rents can be lower under this arrangement because the Corporation has only regular lease payments to make and has no large lump-sum burden.

6

New Directions for Public Finance

Full Use of Fiscal Expenditure
and the Tax System

Building a new Japan through industrial relocation and infrastructure improvement will not be a practical proposition unless large sums of money are invested in imaginative and innovative programs. The necessary funding and creativity will be generated only when we depart from existing laws and institutions to develop an entirely new and daring approach.

Public finance has played a predominant role in Japan's progress over the past one hundred years. While it will continue to be important in the future, its real effectiveness in nation-building will depend upon how far-sighted we are in making priority-oriented fiscal investment. Stopgap fiscal investment made only in response to the consequences of previous actions would simply mean a heavier drain on our financial resources.

Ingenious funding can create the capital necessary for such far-sighted, priority-oriented fiscal investment. One case in point is the toll-road system. When the toll-road concept was first suggested, opponents argued that roads should be free and open for unrestricted public use. In rebuttal, I pointed out that while the road should be free when only one route is available between two points, the availability of parallel routes enables us to legitimately charge for the use of at least one of them. My argument prevailed, and legislative action was taken to build toll roads. Government must always look far ahead and prepare new institutions and new systems for the new age.

Along with the pump-priming function of public finance, I wish to emphasize the positive use of the adjustment mechanism of taxation for policy purposes, specifically to either deter or induce certain activities.

As noted earlier, fiscal expenditures have been, over the past hundred years, the major tool of government policy. However, this is a tool which is typically effective for developing countries. The tax system should be given a much greater role to play in the remodeling of the Japanese archipelago. No longer should the government be the primary promoter of development. The private sector should be called upon to contribute its energy and resources as well. Increased fiscal expenditures and innovative utilization of the taxation system are to be two main pillars for remodeling Japan.

A new motor vehicle weight tax and a factory expulsion tax for overcrowded cities are two of the concrete suggestions that I have proposed on the basis of this new approach.

In order to utilize private energy, those public operations that are profitable can be transferred either to the private sector or to a third sector of cooperation between the private and public sectors. More private capital can be channeled into public works by making active use of the interest-supplement system. This would clearly impose less of a financial burden on the government than direct fiscal investment.

Air, rail, and road transport must be drastically improved so that no place in Japan is more than one day's journey from any other. Blueprints are being drawn for new networks of highways and high-speed railways, as well as for bridges spanning the Inland Sea and connecting Shikoku to the main island of Honshu. The proposed new motor vehicle weight tax is a means to generate funds for such projects.

Motor vehicle owners pay this tax when they acquire a new vehicle and then periodically after that as part of the compulsory vehicle inspection. Since it is a special-purpose tax, the revenue generated is used exclusively for road and railway construction. Opposition is voiced to this tax, but those opposed should remember the earlier controversy about the gasoline tax.

The gasoline tax, when it was first proposed in 1952, met strong resistance on the grounds that special-purpose taxes are an unconstitutional infringement on the Cabinet's right to formulate budget proposals. But today no one questions the "Temporary Measures Law Concerning Funds, etc., of Expenses for Road Improvement," which specifically provides that the Government is to allocate an amount at least equal to gasoline tax revenues for road construction. No longer is this provision challenged, and, furthermore, it has set the precedent for many additional special-purpose taxes.

What was the effect of this tax? The number of motor vehicles in Japan was about 1.3 million in 1952. It has now increased to approximately twenty million. What happened was that the revenue from the gasoline tax promoted the construction of new roads and highways, which in turn stimulated greater motor vehicle production and consequently still greater tax revenues. A similar effect can be expected from the newly proposed motor vehicle weight tax. No matter how fast they may be built, roads alone cannot cope with the sharply increasing demand for freight and passenger transport capacity. Besides, roads would be so congested that vehicles would not be able to move. The only practical solution is to add a vast network of railways for mass transportation. Super-express railways must be constructed throughout the country, primarily for passenger transportation, so that current lines may take on added freight. It is also necessary for these super-express railways to carry freight.

What is involved here is a new approach to roads, railways, and ports as integral parts of the whole. Roads, railways, and ports are all in the same system. Given this approach, it is legitimate to use the revenue from the motor vehicle weight tax for the construction of railways, because motor vehicles will benefit from improved railway transportation.

One controversial point about this tax was that it violates the principle of fair taxation. Needless to say this principle must be observed. But the question of what is fair and the adjustment mechanism of taxation are two problems of entirely different dimensions.

It is widely known that West Germany depends heavily on taxation in building an effective transportation system. If truckers were to roam about the nation's roads with loads too heavy for the roads' physical limits, on the strength of the constitutional guarantee of freedom of business, they would soon ruin the pavement. It is, therefore, essential that railways carry the heavier freight and ships carry the still heavier cargo.

Let us take, for example, the case of a six-ton truck. In Japan, the annual tax is something over $330. In West Germany, the tax on similar trucks is as much as $5,350. This tax is clearly intended to deter people from owning such trucks and to induce them to use railways or ships to transport heavy goods. The beauty of this system is that, by attacking the problem through the tax route, it always leaves room for those who want to carry heavy goods by truck to do so, provided they pay the tax. And the constitutional guarantee of freedom of business is preserved.

Departure from Past Industrial Policy

Industrial relocation is the key to building a new Japan. The pivot for achieving this must be the effective application of the tax system's adjustment mechanism. In other words, an extra tax burden should be imposed on plants and factories located in overcrowded and polluted areas to encourage them to move to less-populated areas. From the point of view of the individual company, there are considerable advantages of economic concentration that come from locating in an industrially crowded area. But from a macro-economic perspective, the drawbacks of aggregation and concentration have created many problems which now outweigh the advantages. Firms which benefit from agglomeration should be specially taxed to arrest the trend toward concentration and to encourage relocation and dispersion to local areas.

On the other hand, companies relocating or building new plants in areas outside of the Pacific industrial belt should be rewarded with tax privileges, such as long-term exemption from property taxes, and special subsidies. Local governments should be compensated by the national government through additional grants for the revenue lost from the application of this preferential taxation. Such subsidies can be financed by the tax revenues that accrue from overcrowded areas, and a special account in the national budget should probably be established for this.

In effect, this means introducing a system of deterrence and inducement taxes, and as such represents a radical departure from the traditional government policy of acquiescing in industrial concentration.

When policy programs for fiscal 1972 were discussed, I proposed the creation of such a tax system. The proposal involved the utilization of the corporate tax surcharge currently set at 1.75 percent. It specifically called for abolishing the corporate tax surcharge from April of 1972, except for income arising from plants and factories operating in overcrowded areas, and raising the tax rate from 1.75 percent to 3.5 percent for income accruing from new plants constructed in such overcrowded areas. The revenue from this tax would then be assigned to a special account which would finance subsidies for industrial relocation and industrial park construction, as well as finance the establishment of the Industrial Relocation and Coal Mining Area Development Corporation. Plants moving out of Industrial Departure Promotion Areas would be given partial or whole property tax exemptions for the first twenty-five years, with the resultant drop in local government revenue to be offset with a subsidy from the special account.

Unfortunately, the recession in the Japanese economy and the "dollar shock" stood in the way of this new policy. Government revenue was expected to decline and, to my chagrin, there was no alternative but to continue the 1.75 percent corporate income tax surcharge for another two years.

But the program of industrial relocation had to be put into effect as quickly as possible. We could not let even one year go to waste. Therefore, I proposed implementing, from fiscal 1972 on, subsidies and interest supplements related to redistribution, using, for example, available funds in the general account. So I promptly reorganized the Coal Mining Area Development Corporation into a new Industrial Relocation and Coal Mining Area Development Corporation, in compliance with the government's policy of restricting creation of new public corporations. Action was also taken to implement a property tax exemption for relocating firms, this exemption to be for the first three years for the time being. This particular measure obviously must be further reexamined taking into account the amount of subsidies needed for local governments.

Thus, though on a provisional basis, the industrial relocation program did get started in 1972. As business recovers, I will look into some additional sources of revenue, including utilization of the corporate tax surcharge. In a way, this might be called a "second gasoline tax." I am just as determined to see this tax implemented and will push this just as vigorously and tenaciously as I did the first gasoline tax.

After World War II, England started with a grand program of rebuilding London under the New Town Act. After a quarter of a century, the job is not yet completed. Brazil's Brasilia project still has some time to go until its real impact can be felt.

The challenge facing Japan is several hundred times larger than London's or Brasilia's. My proposal may not be readily appreciated, but someone must lead the nation in building a new country.

A Design for Greater Public Participation

Until a few years ago, people used to say that money spent for local development was a direct loss to metropolitan areas. But today, most people agree that something must be done to prevent the further inflow of people into our large cities. As certain as water flowing downward, man ever seeks newer heights. People congregate in places which have higher cultural sophistication and social benefits.

So is it with industry. We must build an infrastructure for production when land, water, labor, and power are available and in stable supply, and must create transportation and communication networks that will permit industries to viably locate outside of Tokyo or Osaka.

In order to create such an environment, the government must concentrate its limited financial resources in a pump-priming way in those areas where it has responsibility. This is also true for remodeling big cities.

Whether developing local areas or remodeling cities, the problems are too large for either private or public sector to tackle alone. But enormous energy can be elicited by skillfully maneuvering and utilizing private money, technology, and vitality through effective employment of tax or interest-supplement policies.

For this, the government must identify its area of primary responsibility and do what must be done. Depending upon the degree of public benefit and profitability of operation, the remaining areas can be tackled either by joint efforts of private and public sectors or by private initiative with proper governmental guidance and assistance. The need is to combine private and public efforts in various new patterns of cooperation.

The third sector, joint private-public effort, has become an active participant in local development, and its advantages and disadvantages are now becoming clear. A large-scale third sector is being formed as the principal agent for constructing large industrial parks. The Hokkaido-Tohoku Development Corporation and Mutsu-Ogawara Development Corporation, jointly financed by Aomori Prefecture and private business, are representative examples. Another third sector example, the East Tomakomai Development Corporation, is soon to be inaugurated, and this approach is also being studied for the development of the Shibushi Bay area.

The third sector is also being formed for the construction of large-scale inland industrial parks and distribution centers. The Hokkaido-Tohoku Development Corporation, cited above, is one of these, while the Iwate Development Corporation, in which Iwate Prefecture has been joined by Mitsui-, Mitsubishi-, and Sumitomo-group developers, is another.

There is certainly room for study and improvement in the third-sector type of cooperation, particularly in the area of financing and public representation in its operation. But this is a new pattern worthy of attention, and it should be carefully nurtured.

Involving private resources in the effort to build a new country is the very large task lying ahead of us, and we should take advantage of the abundance of overseas examples and experiences, such as New York's slum-clearance projects mentioned earlier.

Another interesting concept deserving study is that of the workers' housing development in Italy, where surpluses accumulated by life and casualty insurance companies are earmarked exclusively for constructing workers' housing. These restrictions on the use of insurance funds are balanced by such privileges as a twenty-five-year exemption from property taxes and the use of state-owned land free of charge. Originally implemented during Mussolini's time, this policy has been continued by postwar governments.

Common to both examples is the adroit combination of restriction and privilege. Unless restrictions and privileges are in balance, we cannot expect really effective implementation of any program. As we attempt to involve private developers in the huge task of remodeling the Japanese archipelago, such incentives as financial assistance and tax privileges must be adequately balanced by proper governmental guidance and controls.

The involvement of private funds must be seriously studied along with the participation of private developers. Interest supplement is a powerful lever for attracting private money. If money from insurance funds, trust funds, and agricultural cooperatives can be made available for the building of a new Japan, this should provide an extra margin of strength.

Birth of a New Japan

Those born in the Meiji (1868–1912) and the Taisho (1912–1926) Eras have a deep sense of love and pride in their native locales. While life in these rural villages may not have been rich, it was home. Home was the place where your stern father and gentle mother lived, where you could always find your childhood friends, and whose green fields, rolling hills, and fresh streams remained with you forever. Seeking their fortunes, village youths left their ancestral homes for far-away cities where they studied, worked, married, and followed the course of their lives. Saisei Muroo, a poet of those day, sang in praise of his homeplace, "It is where my mind travels from afar." Whatever their fate, whether in success or failure, they always remembered the people and scenes of their unchanging homeplace.

I believe that the endless fountain of energy which has built today's Japan derives from the cherished and respected rural homes from which all of us have originally come.

In this great enterprise of remodeling the Japanese archipelago, I am motivated by a strong desire to rebuild the home of the Japanese people, which has been lost and destroyed and is declining today but which, once restored, will again give to our society a sense of tranquility and spiritual enrichment.

It is true that the urban concentration of both people and production has been the driving force in building today's prosperity. The process of this massive flow has given rise to many whose only home is a two-room apartment in a big city, sapped the villages of their youth, and left behind only the aged and housewives to sweat and toil in back-breaking labor. How can such a society generate the energy necessary to build a new Japan in the next hundred years?

It is such considerations as these that have impelled me to work on the policy of "dispersion" to reverse the tide of people, money, and goods and to create a flow from urban concentrations back to outlying areas, using industrial relocation and the nation-wide communication and transportation networks as the main tools.

This plan for building a new Japan is a set of policy programs to solve simultaneously both overcrowding and underpopulation through the relocation of people and industry into less populated areas. It is, more importantly, an action program to implement these prescribed solutions.

I wish to activate the dynamo of our nation's powers to revitalize the declining rural areas of Japan. By moving pollution-free industries from large cities to outlying areas, local cities can be made strategic cores of development with improved income opportunities. Educational, medical, cultural, and leisure facilities will be adequately provided to enrich the local life environment. Those leaving the farm will find new jobs in local factories and stores, while still being able to cultivate enough land to produce some rice and vegetables for their own consumption. Land they do not need can be leased for salaried cultivation. No longer will they have to leave their villages to seek seasonal employment in the large cities.

Japanese farms of 50 to 75 acres will be mechanically cultivated by a small number of highly efficient farmers raising stock in spacious pastures, growing fruit and rice in well-tended fields and paddies.

Life in the large cities will also be improved. By relocating those industries and universities no longer needed in big cities, urban areas will be freed of pollution and high costs and made comfortable places to live in. City dwellers will work five days a week at worthwhile jobs. While they will live in apartments near their work in their twenties and thirties when they are in the prime of life, in their forties they will have homes in suburbia where they can take care of their aged parents. On weekends, they may enjoy family outings by car to nearby mountains, rivers, or beaches, or they may choose to engage in do-it-yourself carpentry or agriculture in their spare time.

Only when life in both metropolitan and rural Japan is reshaped into one humane, livable environment will the people take pride in their own communities and develop a strong sense of solidarity and mutual cooperation. So long as the people can enjoy the same conveniences and opportunities for self-development wherever they may live, their love for their homeplaces will be firmly restored and will develop into an abiding love of their homeland Japan.

The road before us is steep and rocky. Yet both the necessary funds and ingenuity for this great enterprise can be found if we remain a peace-loving nation and if, on the strength of our high growth potential, we manage our economy to make growth and welfare compatible.

If we join together to consolidate the energy, wisdom, and technology that enabled us to construct today's Japan from the ashes of World War II, I am confident that it is possible to bring about a new era, a renaissance in which man and sunshine and verdant surroundings will replace big cities and industries as the rightful master of society. Japan will indeed be in the vanguard of civilization when the more than one hundred million intelligent and hard-working Japanese people put all of their strength together to solve the problems of inflation, pollution, overcrowding, depopulation, agricultural stagnation, and generation gaps common to all developed countries, and do this without following the path to militarism. As a free nation which knows no social prejudice, which gives its citizens every opportunity for success if they are creative and work hard, Japan will be a trusted and respected member of the international community and will enjoy fraternal relations with all nations regardless of ideological differences.

For the past twenty-five years, I have done my best as a statesman to make Japan a well-balanced, comfortable place to live in. And I shall dedicate the remainder of my life to the consummation of this task. A society where every home is filled with laughter, where senior citizens live peaceful, restful lives, where the eyes of youth shine bright with the light of hope—such is my dream for remodeling the Japanese archipelago.

COMMENTARY

Kakuei Tanaka and
His *Building a New Japan*

By Masumi Muramatsu
Executive Director
Simul International, Inc.

This book is an unabridged translation of Kakuei Tanaka's million-seller *Nippon Retto Kaizo-Ron* in which Japan's young Prime Minister, nicknamed "the Computerized Bulldozer," sets forth his ideas about "remodeling the Japanese archipelago."

Tanaka became Prime Minister in July, 1972, in response to popular demand for a change away from the politics of stagnation and inertia of conservative, bureaucratic administrations. Moving with lightning speed, he visited the People's Republic of China, firmly shook hands with Mao Tse-tung and Chou En-lai, and achieved, a mere four months after taking office, the normalization of Sino-Japanese diplomatic relations, which had long been pending and ardently desired by the Japanese people. His trip to Peking was an epochal event in the history of Japan and of the world. Especially for Japan it marked the beginning of a new age.

In June, 1972, just before assuming the prime-ministership, Tanaka presented his vision of sweeping measures to solve the many contradictions and imbalances that have resulted from prodigious, super-rapid economic growth and for the building of a more livable Japan. This vision constitutes the book *Nippon Retto Kaizo-Ron*.

Background for a Million-Seller

In the quarter century since the end of World War II, Japan has regenerated itself from a land devastated by war to a leader of nations once again. On the other side of the picture, however, rapid economic growth has taken its toll: overconcentration of people and industry in the large cities and, conversely, underpopulation and stagnation in the countryside; pollution of land, air, and water; and inadequate public welfare. Although these are problems that most advanced industrial countries have in common, in Japan's case the need for reform in the socio-economic structure is particularly urgent.

Nippon Retto Kaizo-Ron, published at just such a time, has met with an immediate and explosive reaction at home and with considerable foreign interest as well, inevitably accompanied by argument over the pros and cons of the ideas presented in it. The book conceives the idea of remodeling the whole country into a more livable Japan by rechanneling the flow of population and economic activity, relocating industry, expanding transportation and communications networks, and making full use of mobility and flexibility in fiscal policy implementation. It has today become a focal point of debate among the people at large.

First, the Commission for Remodeling the Japanese Archipelago, made up of prominent leaders in business, labor, government, scholarship, and other fields, got under way as a personal advisory body to the Prime Minister. Then Japan's powerful bureaucratic machinery moved into action. The Ministry of Finance compiled a large-scale, expansionary budget for fiscal 1973 that topped the previous year's by almost 30 percent. The Ministry of International Trade and Industry got started on the job of demarcating the areas from which movement of industry is to be promoted and to which industry is to be attracted as the first step in the industrial relocation plan. The Economic Planning Agency started work on drawing up a comprehensive plan for the use of the national land space. The Ministry of Construction got busy speeding up its plans for construction of new automobile expressways. And a brand new administrative agency is scheduled to make its appearance soon: the National

Commentary

Land Development Agency. Thus, the ideas set forth in this book are being put into action, and the remodeling of Japanese society and national land space is actually in progress.

Why This Had to be Published

When Japan left the League of Nations in 1933, it parted company with the democratic forces in world politics. After that, it passed through an unsavory period of World War II ending with Hiroshima and Nagasaki. Japan's relations with the outside world had long been those not of goodwill and understanding but of displeasure and indifference. Today, however, it has become a world power on the basis of its economic development. An era has arrived in which Japan must bear the serious responsibilities that go along with being one of the leading countries of the world. Whether one likes it or not, Japan's position is now such that the people of the world must learn about the country and try to understand it better.

There have been many foreign-language publications dealing with tourism or with traditional arts in Japan, but few accurately and explicitly tell what the Japanese are thinking or trying to do. It is in this sense that *Nippon Retto Kaizo-Ron* is a valuable book. Through it, the reader can get a good feeling for the living Japan of today.

It is for this reason that The Simul Press and Simul International have jointly undertaken the task of translating and publishing this work for the whole world.

Profile of Kakuei Tanaka

Here I should like to give a brief biographical sketch of the author.

Kakuei Tanaka was born on May 4, 1918, in a rural community in Niigata Prefecture, which borders on the Japan Sea in the geographical area known as Hokuriku and which is famous for its rice production and heavy snowfalls. He was the third-born of a seven-child family and the only son.

Unlike most farming community families in those days, the family's

223

main business was not agriculture. His grandfather made his name as a carpenter specializing in building Shinto shrines. His father, Kakuji Tanaka, a trader in horses and cattle, also was in the business of raising carp (a fish prized in Japan as both a delicacy and an object of aesthetic appreciation); he was a man of great ambition, dreaming of a future day when he could have a large ranch in Hokkaido, and, in an effort to improve his stock through breeding, he imported Holstein dairy cattle from Holland. However, the family was by no means well off financially, since, as is usual in this kind of business, the ups and downs were marked and frequent.

It was his mother, Fume, who kept the family going. Commenting on her superior intelligence and outstanding memory, Tanaka's fourth-grade teacher, a Mr. Kanai, said: "It seems to me the boy inherited the best side of both of his parents—his father's entrepreneurship and his mother's brains."

At the age of two, Tanaka came down with diphtheria. He says in his autobiography, *Watakushi no Rirekisho* (*My Personal History*), that he had a high fever and hovered between life and death. His grandmother told the lad that his habit of stuttering was due to that serious illness.

The boy was so frail physically that his mother often worried aloud whether, at that rate, he would live to be a man. Looking back on his childhood, Tanaka later recalled: "I stuttered so badly that I became very shy. I stopped going outside very much and spent most of my time playing indoors. When I did go out once in a while and someone teased me, I would soon resort to fighting out of frustration at not being able to get words out of my mouth in time. I may have been weak, but that didn't stop me from scrapping."

Tanaka's formal education went no farther than the six years of elementary school. Of the approximately forty prime ministers since Hirobumi Ito took office in 1885 after the parliamentary system was introduced into Japan, almost all were either bureaucrats who had graduated from national university or military men who had graduated from a military academy, with the exception of the elderly statesmen who had played an active role in the early Meiji period. As the *Economist* notes Tanaka is the first one who did not graduate from a university and who worked his way up from poverty.

In rural Japan before World War II, it was quite normal for boys to start working after they finished elementary school. When Tanaka left school in the midst of the Depression, he found he had to start working right away. Despite his excellent record, his first job was as a common laborer pushing rail cars at construction sites.

His scholarly ambitions, however, were not to be put off. The next year, 1934, at the age of fifteen, he left home for Tokyo and settled down for a while at the Tokyo branch of a construction firm called Inoue Kogyo. This marked the beginning of his eventful life in Tokyo. First of all, he went to a civil engineering school at night while working days as a live-in apprentice at Inoue Kogyo. Next, he received on-the-job training as a reporter for an insurance trade journal. After that he worked for a while in the office of a sundry goods importer and then in an architect's office, during which time he continued his studies. In the spring of 1937, a mere nineteen, he started his own one-man business: the Kyoei Construction Office. His work was to draw up building plans for factories and dormitories and to select and supervise subcontractors—quite a job for one man.

In 1939, however, he was drafted and sent to the part of China then known as Manchuria, where he contracted croupous pneumonia and dry pleurisy at the same time. This got him out of the military after two years of service. Except for this interruption, he devoted himself to his construction business, and by 1943 his office, which was to become a joint-stock company in that year with the new name Tanaka Construction Industries, Co., Ltd., had grown into one of the fifty largest construction firms in Japan. This was a most turbulent period in Japanese history, covering the "Manchurian Incident," the wider Pacific War, the fall of Japanese militarism, and finally the rebirth of Japan as a democracy.

Brought up in the snowbound environment of a small rural community, Tanaka worked his way up from the construction sites of Tokyo against great adversity. He set himself a timetable and refused to cling to the past once he had moved on to the next stage. Such a life style accounts in no small measure for the fact that his is a way of thinking at one with the common man and a vitality guided by careful calculation.

*

Tanaka had not considered becoming a politician until 1946 when, at the age of twenty-seven, he decided to run for a Niigata seat in the first House of Representatives election in postwar Japan. As an official candidate of the Progressive Party (later reorganized into the Democratic Party, which still later joined with the Liberal Party to form the Liberal Democratic Party of today), his conviction was that liberal democracy was needed in order to build a new Japan from the ruins of defeat. The result was failure: he was first runner-up. The next year, however, when the House of Representatives was dissolved for the establishment of a new political order before the new Constitution went into effect, Tanaka jumped at this second chance and won. At the age of twenty-eight, he thus secured the House of Representatives seat which he has held through eleven elections to date.

After becoming a member of the Diet, Tanaka gradually moved to the fore of the political scene. Starting with assumption of the position of Minister of Postal Services in 1957, he served under three prime ministers (Kishi, Ikeda, and Sato), as Chairman of the Policy Affairs Research Council of the Liberal Democratic Party (one term), Chief Secretary of the LDP (five terms), Minister of Finance (three terms), Minister of International Trade and Industry (one term), and in other important capacities, during which time he displayed great political prowess while constantly remaining within the conservative mainstream.

Particularly notable among his political achievements have been his management of ratification of the Okinawa reversion agreement while a principal member of the Sato administration as it set a record for the longest-run in Japan's history and his leadership role in the 1969 election when the LDP won over 300 of the 490-some House of Representatives seats.

In 1972, Tanaka, who had become the most influential man in the LDP, defeated Takeo Miki (presently Director Generalof the Environment Agency), Masayoshi Ohira (Minister of Foreign Affairs), and Takeo Fukuda (Director General of the Administrative Management Agency) in an LDP election to become the party's new leader, and soon afterward he was named Prime Minister by the Diet. The party's choice was no doubt decisively influenced by the hope that his fast decisions, bold action, imaginative policies, and common touch would be able to stem the ebb of LDP support, particularly in the cities.

In Publishing This English Edition

In translating, we have made every effort to retain both the content and style of the original text. For the convenience of the reader, however, we have converted metric figures to their English equivalents and monetary sums to U.S. dollars, using the expedient exchange rate of ¥300 to the dollar (which approximates the ¥308 rate prior to the February, 1973, float). As for the names of organizations, groups, laws, and the like, we have used the names that are generally accepted in English-language writing in Japan today. We have also dispensed with some illustrations and photographs in the Japanese edition deemed unnecessary for readers of the English version while furnishing supplementary materials when necessary.

Acknowledgement is made here of the collaboration of Prof. Tasuku Asano, Mr. Frederick M. Uleman, Mr. Masaomi Kondo, Mrs. Hiroko Omori, Mrs. Yoshiko Yonekura, Mrs. Chie Kondo, Mr. Eiichi Ishikawa, Mr. Takamichi Kojima, and many other colleagues and friends in the translation and publication of this book, of the instructive advice offered by Mr. Garrett Scalera (Hudson Institute) and Mr. Bernard Krisher (*Newsweek* Tokyo Bureau Chief) after reading the manuscript of the translation, and of the invaluable assistance extended by Prof. Mitsuko Saito of International Christian University (also Advisor to Simul International) and my colleague Mr. Tatsuya Komatsu.

My heartfelt thanks go to Mr. Katsuo Tamura, Executive Director and Editor-in-Chief of The Simul Press—one of the most outstanding editors on the Japanese publishing scene today—who promoted this project and displayed great professional skill and leadership, and to his highly efficient staff—Miss Eiko Ikuta, Mr. Daitaro Suwabe, Mr. Hirotaka Ota, and Miss Masako Miyoshi—for their enthusiastic constribution.

I know of no words to adequately express the deep gratitude I feel toward all these people.

In the six years that it has been in operation, The Simul Press, aiming at bridging the gap between Japan and the rest of the world, has earned a reputation as the publishing house in Japan with the best journalistic sense and the soundest judgement of what problems are of most interest to Japanese readers. And Simul International, Inc., with its high quality of simultaneous interpretation and its unique ability to provide other services required for international conferences, is the only organization in Japan enjoying the full confidence of its clients in this area of facilitating communication between Japan and other nations.

Last, but certainly not least, I should like to extend my thanks to the author, Mr. Kakuei Tanaka, who so readily granted The Simul Press all foreign-language translation and publishing rights, and also Mr. Toshio Shirai, President of the Nikkan Kogyo Shimbun Ltd., the publisher of the original Japanese edition.

(Tokyo, April 1973)

THE SIMUL PRESS IDEAL

The Simul Press, Inc., was launched with the aim of developing international publishing activities from a posture of participating with readers in creating the history of our convulsive times.

Mankind has ceaselessly waged war in pursuit of peace and divided against itself while wishing that the world were one. Scientific advances have brought about an electronic-communication era. But the very simultaneity of information availability tends to bring about identical and simplistic responses all over the world, in turn subjecting mankind to the distress of yet new misunderstanding.

To remove the roots of conflict spawned by such misunderstanding and to enrich international qualities of Japan, once again a leader of nations, we present the raw materials, both from the past and the present, which will help identify various domestic issues as well as deepen international understanding. It is our earnest wish that through our efforts we may contribute to recovering the essential conditions of humanity and unifying all peoples as one world in peace.

May this humble yet lofty ideal to which we dedicate ourselves be blessed with the support of our readers.

SIMUL'S LONG-RUN SELLERS

SIMUL "Issues of Japan" Series

- ■ **Japan—A Punchbag of the World,** Yasuo Takeyama
- □ **The Fragile Blossom,** Z. Brzezinski
- □ **Japan: The Govt.-Business Relationship,** U.S. Commerce Dept.
- ■ **Scarred Japan,** ed. The Asahi Shimbun
- ■ **Religions in Japan,** Yukio Hisaki

SIMUL "Documentary" Series

- □ **The Pentagon Papers,** ed. The New York Times
- □ **Hô Chi Minh,** J. Lacouture
- ■ **The Ugly Japanese,** Masahide Ota
- □ **American in Disguise,** D. I. Okimoto
- ■ **Okinawa and Me,** Shui Ikemiyagi
- □ **Prime Time: The Life of E. R. Murrow,** A. Kendrick

SIMUL "Theses" Series

- □ **The Academic Revolution,** D. Riesman, C. Jencks
- □ **Social Mobility in Industrial Society,** S. M. Lipset, R. Bendix
- □ **Images of Asia,** H. R. Isaacs
- □ **Society and Education in Japan,** H. Passin
- □ **Election Campaigning Japanese Style,** G. L. Curtis
- □ **Mirror for Man,** C. Kluckhohn
- □ **Le Conflit Israélo-Arabe,** ed. J-P. Sartre
- □ **Le Péché Monétaire de l'Occident,** J. Rueff
- □ **The Corporate Oligarch,** D. Finn

SIMUL "Essay" Series

- □ **The Crazy Ape** *and* **What Next?,** A. Szent-Györgyi
- □ **America and Americans,** J. Steinbeck
- □ **La Rivoluzione Culturale in Cina,** A. Moravia

SIMUL "Communication" Series

- ■ **English Works for You,** Masao Kunihiro
- ■ **Science of Spoken Language,** Mitsuko Saito
- ■ **Understanding Misunderstanding,** Sen Nishiyama
- ■ **Communications Gap Between Japan and the U. S.,**
  ed. Yonosuke Nagai, H. Rosovsky

(□ Translations, all in Japanese)